T0342397

Institutional and Organizational Economics

To my parents Grete and Jan
and my wife Lisa

Institutional and Organizational Economics

A Behavioral Game Theory
Introduction

Tore Ellingsen

polity

Copyright © Tore Ellingsen 2024

The right of Tore Ellingsen to be identified as Author of this Work has been asserted in accordance with the UK Copyright, Designs and Patents Act 1988.

First published in 2024 by Polity Press

Polity Press
65 Bridge Street
Cambridge CB2 1UR, UK

Polity Press
111 River Street
Hoboken, NJ 07030, USA

All rights reserved. Except for the quotation of short passages for the purpose of criticism and review, no part of this publication may be reproduced, stored in a retrieval system or transmitted, in any form or by any means, electronic, mechanical, photocopying, recording or otherwise, without the prior permission of the publisher.

ISBN-13: 978-1-5095-5899-5 (hardback)
ISBN-13: 978-1-5095-5900-8 (paperback)

A catalogue record for this book is available from the British Library.

Library of Congress Control Number: 2023932485

Typeset in 10.5 on 13pt Sabon LT Pro
by Cheshire Typesetting Ltd, Cuddington, Cheshire
Printed and bound by CPI Group (UK) Ltd, Croydon, CR0 4YY

The publisher has used its best endeavors to ensure that the URLs for external websites referred to in this book are correct and active at the time of going to press. However, the publisher has no responsibility for the websites and can make no guarantee that a site will remain live or that the content is or will remain appropriate.

Every effort has been made to trace all copyright holders, but if any have been overlooked the publisher will be pleased to include any necessary credits in any subsequent reprint or edition.

For further information on Polity, visit our website:
politybooks.com

Contents

Preface

The book's title echoes the name of an academic association I recently had the honor to preside over: Society for Institutional and Organizational Economics (SIOE).[1] Members of SIOE come from all parts of social science, including economics, management, political science, law, and sociology. My hope is that the same will be true of the book's readers.

Leading academic journals are full of institutional and organizational economics. Yet, there are few university courses with this focus. Perhaps a new textbook will encourage more teachers to create one. In addition, I hope the book can be helpful as complementary reading in other courses – just as many of SIOE's members see our yearly conference as their *second* conference.

The book is meant to be self-contained. A patient and talented high-school student could absorb everything without consulting other sources. That said, the text sometimes investigates difficult issues and leaves out a lot of detail.

---

[1] The society was founded in 1997 under the name International Society for New Institutional Economics (ISNIE). The name changed in 2015. https://sioe.org.

Even experienced social scientists are likely to find some challenging and unfamiliar ideas. For the benefit of curious readers who want to know more as well as advanced readers wanting to check the logical coherence and empirical basis of my claims, I have included a closing chapter with pointers to relevant readings.

Chapters 1–5 are easiest. Chapters 12–15 are too hard for an intro class. My 3rd-year economics BSc students enjoy the whole book, as do MSc and PhD students. Or so they say.

A message to students: As you progress through the book, you will need to absorb quite a bit of "behavioral game theory." If you have never come across it before, it may feel intimidating. But please don't be put off. It's both simpler and more practically relevant than it first seems.

A message to teachers: This book is concise. I have included some exercises, stories, and food for thought, but your students might demand more. On my home page, I will maintain a repository of lecture slides (using Latex Beamer). Upon request, if you give a course, I will also share some additional exercises and solutions for them.

There are more comments to make and a long list of people to thank. But you will better understand my gratitude if you have first had a look at the book's substance, so I leave further meta-comments to the Postface.

1

The Organizational Challenge

Some countries are peaceful and prosperous. Others are hostile and poor.

Why do some countries succeed while others fail?[1]

Why are some firms profitable while others in the same business make losses?

Why do some marriages prosper while others end in divorce?

At first sight, the three questions may seem completely unrelated. The success and failure of countries is the domain of political science. The success and failure of firms is the domain of management science. The success and failure of marriages is the domain of psychology and folklore.

Yet, countries, firms, and marriages have one thing in common: They comprise more than one individual. Therefore, they all face the same organizational challenge: *How can people be made to help rather than hurt each other?*

---

[1] Do you want to know what has been written about this exact topic? For the most part, I refrain from giving references to academic research in the main text. However, in Chapter 20 I offer some pointers to the relevant literature you may want to consult.

The organizational challenge existed long before we had countries, firms, and marriages. It existed before our ancestors became human.

Answers to the challenge usually contain at least one of the following three elements.

- **Sacrifice:** Individuals voluntarily make sacrifices for others.
- **Cooperation:** Individuals coordinate their actions for mutual benefit.
- **Coercion:** Individuals are forced to take actions that benefit others.

Our task is to understand how desirable sacrifice, cooperation, and coercion come about. I cannot promise to deliver a definite answer. But I can promise to share with you a powerful language for discussing possible answers: the language of behavioral game theory.

The meaning of success depends on the group we consider. For example, two families can each be successful in the sense that family members cooperate well with each other in serving the family's goals. Yet, if a large fraction of each family's resources is used for the purpose of fighting against the other family, then the society comprising both families is not successful. The cooperation that is valuable at one level can be harmful at other levels.

A noteworthy example is due to Banfield (1958), who makes a detailed study of the life in Chiaromonte, a small town in Southern Italy. He observes that nepotism and corruption is widespread, as people give priority to their families over the community at large. As a result, Banfield argues, the town is underdeveloped. In a broader empirical study, Putnam (1993) addresses Banfield's argument by comparing different parts of Italy. Putnam documents that the more prosperous regions in the North tend to have more extensive traditions of community-wide and non-hierarchical associations, such as guilds, clubs, and choirs.

More generally, people in the North behave less selfishly

and more in line with the broader social interest. As a result, there is less need for regulation. Also, the regulators themselves behave less selfishly. When business partners and regulators are trustworthy, entrepreneurs dare to invest, and investment leads to prosperity.[2] Likewise, firms function better when employees can trust their employers and vice versa. Political philosopher John Stuart Mill expressed it well:

> The moral qualities of the labourers are fully as important to the efficiency and worth of their labour, as the intellectual [...] The advantage of humankind of being able to trust one another penetrates into every crevice and cranny of human life: the economical is perhaps the smallest part of it, yet even this is incalculable.
>
> (Mill, 1848, Vol. I, Book I, Ch. VII, para. 5)

But just as strong families can constitute a problem for their town when they engage in feuds and nepotism, strong towns and countries can cause problems for the wider world. For example, it might not have been a coincidence that the rise of the Nazi party was most rapid and extensive in the parts of Germany that were rich in civic associations, including animal breeders, chess clubs, and choirs.[3]

From now on, when we study the relative success of local regions, the relevant group boundary is the local community. When we study the world's ability to deal with global challenges such as climate change, pandemics, or nuclear war, the relevant group boundary is the global population.

The book is primarily theoretical. It provides concepts

---

[2] The original purpose of Putnam's project (which he conducted together with Italian researchers Leonardi and Nanetti) was to study the impacts of Italy's sudden decision – in the spring of 1970 – to decentralize political power. As it turned out, the new local governments were more effective in the North than in the South. In trying to find out why, the researchers came to raise the much larger question of how societies succeed.

[3] This provocative hypothesis is explored by Satyanath, Voigtländer, and Voth (2017).

for thinking systematically about sacrifice, cooperation, and coercion, often by means of stylized examples. Many of these examples involve "societies" comprised of only two parties. The reason is that the fundamental organizational challenge is often the same, regardless of whether situation involves two individuals, two million individuals, or two billion individuals.[4]

[4] There are important exceptions; I mention one in Chapter 12 and one in Chapter 13.

2
Sacrifice

Imagine the following situation: By sacrificing one dollar, you can make sure that another person gets two dollars. What will you do, and why? Please think about the answer for at least half a minute before reading on.[1]

Did you make the sacrifice? Or did you prefer to keep your dollar?

Or maybe you want to object that this question is too imprecise? Maybe you need to know whether you can make a deal with the other person, or at least whether you will engage with the other person again in the future? Or maybe you would just need to know who the other person is? Is it a friend or a stranger, a rich person or a poor person? These are reasonable objections, so let me pose a more precise question.

The Unilateral Sacrifice Experiment: *Both you and the other person take part in an experiment. You do not know who the*

---

[1] The purpose of the book is to practice thinking, not reading or remembering. I believe it will be most enjoyable if you think hard about each question and answer it honestly – at least to yourself.

*other person is, only that he or she sits in another room in the
same building. The experimenter has given you a dollar. The
other person has gotten nothing. You decide whether to give
the dollar or to keep it. If you give it, the experimenter takes
your dollar, adds another dollar, and gives both dollars to the
person in the other room. You will not learn who the other
person was. (The experimenter is only interested in finding
out what motivates behavior, so there is no need to consider
what the experimenter would like you to do.)*

Is this description clear enough? Have you made a choice?
If so, please spend a minute thinking about your reasons for
that choice. How would you explain those reasons to your
best friend? Please write down a one-sentence justification for
your choice before reading on.[2]

Some readers will have decided to keep the dollar. I have a
question for them: *Suppose that by sacrificing your dollar you
would have created a benefit of one thousand dollars for the
other person. Would you still keep it?*

Some readers will have decided to give the dollar. Here
is a question for them. Which of the following reasons best
describe your reasons for giving?

1. I like to make others happy.
2. I feel a duty to do the right thing.

I also have two questions for everyone.

1. Would it make any difference if you knew that the recipient was a family member? A neighbor? A friend? Someone
   of the same (or a different) religion? Someone from the
   same (or a different) political party?

---

[2] If you think my description of the experiment is still not clear enough for
you to make a choice, please make a note of what additional information you
would need.

2. Would it make any difference to your choice if you had to make it in front of friends or family?

On the next pages, we consider two more modifications of the Sacrifice Experiment. Please think carefully about them. You might want to make notes of your thinking next to each example. Later, you may consult those notes to see which theory (if any) can best account for your reasoning.

The Bilateral Sacrifice Experiment. *Suppose now that you, in addition to choosing whether to give a dollar, will also be a recipient. You are matched with one other person. You decide whether to give to that person and that person decides whether to give to you. As before, each gift is multiplied by two.*

Compared to the Unilateral version, are you more or less willing to give the dollar now? If there is a change in your willingness to give, what caused it?

The Multilateral Sacrifice Experiment. *Suppose finally that there are n participants in the experiment, where $n > 2$. For each participant that gives her dollar, each other participant gets $2/(n - 1)$ dollars. That is, everyone but the giver shares two dollars.*

Compared to the Bilateral version, are you more or less willing to give the dollar now? If there is a change in your willingness to give, what caused it? What role does the number n play in your reasoning?[3]

These experiments go to the heart of the social sciences. The last two Sacrifice Experiments are better known as **social dilemmas.** The dilemma is this: Each person is poorer when giving, but all are richer if all give.

Social dilemmas are common. Fishermen at a lake can catch more fish if they all fish responsibly, but regardless of

---

[3] Note that this experiment would be the same as the Bilateral Sacrifice Experiment if $n = 2$.

what the others do, each fisherman catches more fish by fishing irresponsibly. People all over the world would be more secure if every country would cut military expenditures by half, but each country is more secure if it does not. Global warming would be smaller if we all emitted less greenhouse gases, but each one of us may have a personal interest in taking a long-distance flight.

We do not always act selfishly. Many readers will have been willing to sacrifice their dollar in one or more of the sacrifice experiments. Even if you did not, you might have been unselfish in your daily life. Please take a few seconds to refresh your memory: To what extent have you been engaging in the following activities?

- Giving money or time to charitable organizations.
- Helping neighbors, friends, or colleagues without compensation or expectation of help in return.
- Refraining from activities that pollute or destroy the environment or otherwise hurt other people.

Is your behavior in these real-life situations affected by the same kind of motives that influenced your thinking about the Sacrifice experiments? Or are there factors in daily life that are missing from the experiments? If so, what are they?

The willingness to make sacrifices for the benefit of strangers varies strongly across cultures, as is strikingly illustrated by a recent lost-wallet experiment by Cohn et al. (2019).[4] The researchers turned in "lost" wallets containing valuables – including varying amounts of money – at banks, hotels, post offices, and other public and private service providers around the world. In total, the authors deposited over 17,000 wallets in 355 cities in forty countries. The wallets included the owner's email address, allowing the authors to measure the fraction of wallets that were honestly handled

---

[4] The study is available for free here: https://science.sciencemag.org/content/365/6448/70.

at the various places. For wallets containing money, honesty ranged from about 12 percent in Peru to about 80 percent in Denmark and Sweden.

A cross-country experiment on cheating, by Gächter and Schulz (2016), reaches a similar conclusion. The authors let participants roll a die in private and paid them according to the number they reported. In this experiment, it is easy for the participants who happen to roll a low number to earn more money by falsely claiming the number was high. Since they cannot observe the die-rolls, it is impossible for the researchers to identify individual instances of cheating. Yet, because there are many participants in the study, the distribution of claims precisely reveals the average extent of cheating in each country.[5]

The estimated percentage of fully honest participants varies from less than 5 percent in Tanzania to more than 85 percent in Germany. Again, there is a close correlation between cheating in the experiment and broader measures of cheating in the society as a whole, such as measures of corruption and the size of the shadow economy. Since cheating is profitable for the individual, but usually harmful to others, cheating is intimately related to social dilemmas. It is hardly a coincidence that countries suffering from cheating tend to be poorer than countries with more honest populations – although some of the cheating may well be caused by poverty rather than the other way around.

What can societies do to resolve social dilemmas? In principle, there are two distinct solutions. One is to affect people's preferences. Perhaps there is something about the upbringing and education of people in the Nordic countries that makes them behave unselfishly in the lost-wallet experiment and lie less in the die-roll experiment?

The other solution to social dilemmas is to accept that selfishness exists and to organize society in such a way that

---

[5] The die-roll experiment was invented quite recently by Fischbacher and Föllmi-Heusi (2013) and has quickly become the most popular experimental method for studying dishonesty.

the social dilemmas disappear. Perhaps the Nordic countries simply have in place systems for rewarding charitable behavior and punish cheating? Obviously, societies do not have to choose only one solution. Maybe the two solutions work better together than any one of them separately?

In order to think clearly about how to resolve social dilemmas – replacing greed and conflict with sacrifice and cooperation – we need a proper vocabulary. The next three chapters introduce the main concepts we shall use.[6]

---

[6] In case you find it difficult, do not despair. It is likely to be hard in the way that learning to ride a bicycle is hard. Once you get over the unfamiliarity, it becomes a lot easier.

3

Selfishness, Rationality, and Utility

In the previous chapter, I already used a word that needs careful definition: *selfishness*. We say a person is selfish when she lacks kindness toward and responsibility for others.[1]

Let me also take the opportunity to introduce another word: *rationality*. We say a person is rational if she takes actions that are consistent with her goals. Otherwise, she is irrational.

There are three main kinds of irrationality. One is to forget or otherwise neglect the goals one has. It is typically irrational to get heavily drunk the night before an important exam.[2]

A second kind of irrationality is to draw wrong conclusions from the information at hand. In complicated situations, we are all prone to some irrationality, because our cognitive capacity is limited. A perfect human chess player will never

---

[1] According to this definition, a spiteful person (who takes pleasure in others' adversity) is also selfish. However, I mostly ignore spiteful behavior. Caring about relative performance can resemble spite, and is common in practice, but I mostly abstract from status-seeking as well.

[2] There are exceptions. If you are extremely clever, you can perform well enough even with a hangover. If you value partying above all else, you may be willing to give up on the exam in favor of a more ecstatic night out.

exist. However, in this book, we shall only be concerned about systematic kinds of erroneous conclusions. For example, many people are unable to understand how little weight should be attached to new information when we already have a lot of existing information.

The third kind of irrationality is to hold incorrect beliefs for other reasons. Sometimes, we misread ourselves. Many people, especially males, are prone to overestimate their own abilities. Others, often females, underestimate theirs. Sometimes, we misread the external world. For example, during the Coronapandemic some people believed the virus did not actually exist. I will classify such beliefs as irrational even if the people holding them have been fed with misinformation.[3]

According to our definition, a selfish person can be rational or irrational. Likewise, an unselfish person can be rational or irrational.[4]

For centuries, social scientists have thought hard about how to describe rational decision-making in a simple way. For most purposes, the answer is *expected utility theory*. Expected utility theory describes the decision-maker's preferences through a *utility function* and the beliefs through a *probability function*. The decision-maker chooses the action that gives the highest expected utility.[5]

---

[3] As Nunn (2022) reminds us, the distinction between superstition and rationality can be blurry. For example, traditional cooking often involves spices and rituals that have superstitious origins, but science has subsequently shown that the spices and rituals promote health.

[4] By contrast, some authors define rationality as implying selfishness. In my experience, these authors always struggle to give coherent and plausible explanations for unselfish behavior. It's an unhelpful definition. That said, there are many other definitions of rationality in the literature. For example, some authors will define rationality as requiring only consistency and not unbiased beliefs. My definition here is broadly representative of current usage in decision theory.

[5] There is a rich mathematical literature, called measurement theory, which links properties of rankings to properties of functions that can represent those rankings. For risk preferences, the most important representation theorems were proved in the 1940s by John von Neumann and Oskar Morgenstern and in the 1950s by Leonard Savage. The theorems give conditions under which

Do not be confused. Nobody in their right mind thinks that people carry around utility functions that they consciously maximize. Rather, the idea is that if the decision-maker can rank the alternatives she faces in a consistent manner, then the ranking can be described by certain utility and probability functions. And, if she consistently chooses according to that same ranking, the decision-maker behaves *as if* she maximizes expected utility. In this sense, we can even describe the behavior of animals, plants, and other organisms as being rational.

Utility and Desire

For a selfish person i who only cares about their own material consumption, we can describe the preferences by any increasing function $U_i(c_i)$, where U_i denotes person i's utility and c_i denotes person i's consumption. That may sound abstract, but it just means that if consumption is higher, then utility is higher too.

If the person is not entirely selfish, but also cares about others' consumption, then we must include their consumption in the person's utility function also; we may then write it $U_i(c)$, where $c = (c_1, ..., c_n)$ is the consumption of the n people that i cares about.[6] The function then needs to describe how i weighs others' consumption relative to her own consumption. For example, suppose the person's own consumption goes up

there exist utility and probability functions with the property that lotteries can be adequately ranked according to their expected utility. Risk aversion is measured by the curvature of this utility function: When the function is concave, the decision-maker is risk averse; when it is linear, the decision-maker is risk neutral, and when it is convex, the decision-maker is risk seeking.

[6] Don't be intimidated by the notation. The expression $(c_1, ..., c_n)$ is just a list of numbers, with number c_i denoting the consumption of person i. (Such lists are called vectors.) It is useful to have a shorthand notation for such lists and, typically, we simply use the same letter as for the list items, but without the subscript.

by five percent and a friend's consumption goes down by ten percent, does the person's utility go up or down?[7]

If a person makes decisions under uncertainty, the utility function needs to rank consumption lotteries as well as consumption levels. In this book, I simplify whenever I can.[8] Therefore, in the presence of uncertainty I (almost always) assume people maximize the expectation of whatever their objective is. In the terminology of decision theory, we assume people are risk neutral.

Exercise 3.1

1. Write down a simple utility function for a selfish person.
2. Write down a simple utility function for an altruistic person.
3. Write down a simple utility function for a person who loves equality.

Utility and Duty

Economists often assume people care only about consequences. Sociologists object that this assumption is typically wrong; people are also directly concerned about the actions they take. One reason is that society imposes its understandings and values. Teachers and religious leaders actively promote some values and criticize others. Within the family, parents similarly reinforce values they want their kids to

---

[7] If you read a course in economics, the utility function may include many types of consumption instead. For example, when studying food purchases, the utility function includes food and non-food consumption. When studying how much people choose to work, the utility function includes consumption and leisure. When studying savings behavior, the utility function includes consumption at different points in time.

[8] Scholars tend to like this quote by Antoine de Saint-Exupéry (*Wind, Sand, and Stars*, 1939): "Perfection is achieved, not when there is nothing more to add, but when there is nothing left that can be taken away."

hold.[9] Last, but not least, governments impose laws and regulations.

When parents, teachers, or government officials forbid or advise against some action, people may feel bad about taking that action regardless of any sanctions. To represent the desire to obey duties, we consider utility functions of the general form

$$u_i(s) = U_i(c(s)) + \lambda_i v(s), \qquad (3.1)$$

where $s = (s_1, ..., s_n)$ are the actions that relevant people take. We call these actions s (for strategy) rather than a (for action) for reasons that will become clear.

The function v denotes *social values*. It does not have an index i, since social values are determined at the group level. The parameter λ_i indicates the extent to which i cares about social values, i.e., the person's *loyalty* or dutifulness.[10] In general, a person's loyalty to group values might be affected by the perceived *legitimacy* of the imposed values. For example, when a country is occupied or ruled by a tyrant, many people will feel less loyalty to the government's decrees than they do to those of a democratically elected government. However, to keep notation simple we shall mostly treat λ_i as a fixed number here, in which case loyalty is entirely a characteristic of the individual rather than a function of the situation.

The function v may take several forms, but I shall usually imagine that it only takes non-positive values.[11] The idea is that social values are constraining; they get us to do things

---

[9] Parents and teachers might also try to teach genuine concern for other people. For example, a child who is treated with empathy and care might become empathetic and caring.

[10] Please don't be intimidated by the Greek letters. I only use them to distinguish parameters (i.e., numbers) from functions. The Greek letters I use in this book are α (alpha), β (beta), δ (delta), κ (kappa), λ (lambda), π (pi), ρ (rho), τ (tau), φ (phi), and ω (omega).

[11] Why do I say non-positive instead of negative? Because it is natural that the function takes the value 0 when i acts appropriately.

we otherwise might not want to do. Hence, when possible, we might want to avoid situations where such social pressure applies.[12]

When society has clear rules about right and wrong, it is reasonable to assume that the function $v(s)$ jumps down, as s goes from being permitted to being forbidden. For example, in a society where people are supposed to tell the exact truth and not to steal, a moral individual feels guilty about a selfish lie or theft, even if the transgression has little material consequence.

There is a famous saying that *economics is about individuals' choices, sociology about how individuals don't have any choices to make.*[13] Equation 3.1 allows both of these extreme views. When λ goes to infinity, the individual does what society asks. They follow a *logic of appropriateness.* In a society without social pressure, the individual focuses entirely on attaining her own goals.[14] They follow a *logic of consequences.*

Note that under the "standard" economic assumption that people ignore social pressure, we have $u_i(s) = U_i(c(s))$. This formulation still allows altruism and fairness, for example. Only if person i is selfish, do the own goals coincide with the own consumption, or formally $u_i(s) = U_i(c_i(s))$. Unless the society is completely without social pressure or populated

---

[12] There are exceptions. Sometimes, we may enjoy our duties, perhaps because we develop a loyalty to the cause and a stronger sense of belonging to the group that our duties serve. The Enlightenment philosopher David Hume (1751, Section IX, Part II, final paragraph) argues that we are mistaken in trying to evade our duties. In his view, the fulfilment of social duties brings a "peaceful reflection on one's own conduct," which is of more worth than "the feverish, empty amusements of luxury and expense."

[13] The quote is due to James Duesenberry, commenting on a theory by an economist (Gary Becker) of a phenomenon that traditionally belonged outside of economics (human fertility). The year was 1960, but the quote still rings true today.

[14] I do not think such a society exists. Nor do I think many people would want such a society to exist. For example, even libertarians desire that people voluntarily respect each others' liberal rights. But see Footnote 17.

only by people immune to it, both $U(c(s))$ and $v(s)$ matter for understanding behavior, to different degrees.

It is easy to think that in individualistic societies, social pressures are more limited than in collectivistic societies and that people will therefore be inherently more selfish in individualistic societies. However, this is not correct. Rather, collectivistic societies use punishments and rewards to enforce conformism, whereas individualistic societies encourage people to respect others and to be kind. Thus, trust in the kindness of others is greater in individualistic societies than in collectivistic societies.[15] Liberalism is *not* a license to be selfish, neither in theory nor in practice.[16] As an illustration of this point, let me share with you a favorite segment from Torbjørn Egner's liberal children's book *When the Robbers Came to Cardamom Town* from 1955. The Constable is singing about the Law of Cardamom, which is short and simple (my translation from Norwegian):

You should never bother others
You should be forever kind
But beyond that there is nothing more to mind

That is, only when justice and charity have received their dues are you free to do what you want.[17]

---

[15] Chapter 20 provides some references to the extensive literature that has established these findings.

[16] A major purpose of political liberalism in the 18th and 19th centuries was to reduce social pressure and leave people free to pursue their own goals, but not to the detriment of society. The Wikipedia article on Liberalism is informative and highly recommended.

[17] Accordingly, there are philosophers who consider that liberalism is not free enough. For example, Friedrich Nietzsche, in his book *On the Genealogy of Morality* from 1887 argued that it may be a better society that does not seek to limit individuality, regardless of the conflicts that may thereby be created.

Utility and Evolution

Where do preferences come from ultimately? Evolutionary theory posits that behavior will be geared to maximize the reproduction of the organism or, more precisely, the organism's genes. Simple organisms do not consciously make plans, but organisms whose behavior entails larger quantities of own offspring automatically come to constitute a larger fraction of the relevant population.

Similar evolutionary forces can work through the copying of successful individuals' behaviors (memes), rather than merely through genetic replication. Birdsong evolves through such mechanisms, as does apes' use of tools and decorations. Charles Darwin (1871), founder of the theory of evolution, was convinced our moral instincts and feelings of guilt and shame have deep evolutionary roots. In this, he followed moral philosopher Adam Smith, who had articulated similar ideas a century earlier, albeit with great care not to attract the ire of bishops and priests.

Evolutionary theory offers a straightforward explanation for the great sacrifices people are prepared to make for the benefit of family members. We share half of our genes with a (whole) sibling. Biologist J.B.S. Haldane was once asked the question: "Would you sacrifice your life for a fellow human being?" His reply: "No, but for two brothers or eight cousins, yes."

Evolutionary theory also explains why animals can compete intensely for mating opportunities. Risking one's life in order to mate does not help the individual and may not even benefit the species – male frogs sometimes end up killing the female frog that they compete to fertilize – but it could promote one's genes.

Early in history, it is likely that there was competition for resources between groups of humans (and between our earlier ancestors too).[18] Thus, it seems likely that evolutionary

---

[18] To some extent, there are still elements of competition between groups of people, despite our great ability to trade and learn new technologies from each other.

forces may also apply between groups. *Group-selection* refers to the idea that a behavior that is harmful to the individual could be favored by evolution, as long as the behavior helps the individual's group to grow relative to other groups.[19] For example, cultural anthropologists believe that the extended family came to play an important role in parts of China that relied on growing rice, because this is a large-scale activity that cannot be conducted by a nuclear family alone. Thus, these parts of China became more kinship-oriented (clan-based, collectivistic) than the parts of China where wheat was the most important crop.

Externalities

We are now ready to use the concept of "utility" to articulate the conflict between self-interest and group-interest.

When a person's action has an impact on somebody else's utility, we say the action causes an *externality*. For example, when I use my outdoor grill on the balcony or play loud rock music, I impose a *negative externality* on my neighbors in the apartment block, as they would prefer silence and fresh air. If on the other hand I help to keep our communal areas tidy and clean, I contribute a positive externality.

Even when we trade in a market, we cause externalities. When you purchase something, you usually make the seller happy, because the price is higher than the seller's cost.

---

[19] Here is Charles Darwin (1871, Ch. 5) on group selection and moral behavior:

> Ultimately our moral sense or conscience becomes a highly complex sentiment – originating in the social instincts, largely guided by the approbation of our fellowmen, ruled by reason, self-interest and, in later times, by deep religious feelings, and confirmed by instruction and habit. It must not be forgotten that although a high standard of morality gives but a slight or no advantage to each individual man and his children over the other men of the same tribe, yet an increase in the number of well-endowed men and an advancement in the standard of morality will certainly give an immense advantage to one tribe over another.

When you sell something, you usually make the buyer happy, because the price is below the buyer's valuation. Only in the exceptional case of a "perfectly competitive" market is there no externality from a trade, as both the seller's cost and the buyer's valuation coincide with the price.

By the way, must we say grilling creates a negative externality, or might we instead say refraining from grilling creates a positive externality? The answer depends on entitlements. If it is clear that my neighbors are more entitled to fresh air than I am to grill my food on the balcony, then grilling creates a negative externality. If, on the other hand, the right-to-grill is an accepted principle, then refraining from grilling creates a positive externality.

Mostly, we cause negative externalities not because we are evil, but because we are uninformed or unconcerned. When we take a long-distance flight or buy a gas-guzzling car, the impact on others is an unfortunate side-effect, rather than the goal we pursue. Indeed, some of our greatest global challenges are due to a multitude of negative externalities that each is tiny, but which jointly cause large damage.

For example, the problem of CO_2 emissions involves virtually all the people in the world imposing some externality on almost everyone else. It is a truly gigantic social dilemma.[20]

Efficiency

One of the most important words in economics is *efficiency*. An outcome (i.e., a strategy profile s or consequence c) is said to be efficient if there does not exist another outcome that is better (i.e., yields higher utility) for some and is worse for none. Conversely, if there *is* an outcome that is

---

[20] Strictly speaking, it is a bit more complicated than that. Some people and places benefit from global warming, as agricultural yields improve and the local climate becomes more habitable.

better for some and worse for none, then the outcome is *inefficient*.[21]

Social dilemmas, such as the Multilateral Sacrifice Experiment are stark examples. There, if everyone fails to sacrifice, everyone could have been better off if all sacrificed. In short, selfish behavior yields an inefficient outcome in a social dilemma.

What about the Unilateral Sacrifice Experiment, where you can sacrifice one dollar in order for another to earn two dollars – is the outcome inefficient if you fail to sacrifice? Strictly speaking, the answer is no. Sacrifice is good for the other person but, since you are worse off, the sacrifice does not improve efficiency. However, if there were a way for the other person to make a transfer (of anywhere between one and two dollars) to you, not sacrificing is inefficient: Both are then better off if you sacrifice and the other compensates you.

When economists see a dysfunctional organization or society, or an unresolved global challenge, we suspect that inefficiency is involved.

Food for Thought 3.1 *On February 24, 2022, the Russian army invaded Ukraine. In response, the governments of many other countries have supported Ukraine by sending money, goods, and weapons. Explain how this situation represents a social dilemma. What role do you think that altruism and dutifulness play in the help that countries give?*

---

[21] This notion of efficiency is associated with the Italian sociologist Vilfredo Pareto. Hence, we often call it Pareto-efficiency.

4
Situations, Games, and Cooperation

It is fascinating to think about the motives of individuals. But ultimately, what we want to understand here is how societies function. Thus, we must study the *interplay* between individuals. When and why do individuals cooperate? When and why do they end up harming each other instead? What role does unselfishness play? Is it possible for entirely selfish people to find ways to cooperate? What is the role of individual characteristics, and what is the role of group characteristics?

The language of game theory helps us to discuss these kinds of questions in a precise way. A *social situation*, also called a *game form*, comprises three elements:

1. The people involved in the situation (the *players*).
2. The information and actions that are available to them (the *strategies*).
3. The potential results of those actions (the *consequences*).

A *game* is a situation (game form) together with a utility function for each player.

Please read the previous sentence a couple of times until you feel you really understand it. Many unnecessary misunderstandings, even between great scholars, occur because people fail to distinguish between situations and games.

Example: benevolent sacrifice

For example, suppose a player called Rowena finds herself in a Unilateral Sacrifice situation. She is in a position to help another player, called Colin. Help is worth two dollars to Colin and costs Rowena an amount of effort that is worth one dollar to her. Thus, the players in the situation are Rowena and Colin. Rowena knows she can choose to sacrifice for Colin or not. Thus, her two available strategies are to sacrifice (S) and not to sacrifice (N). The consequence if she chooses S can be written (0, 2) and the consequence if she chooses N can be written (1, 0).[1] In each case, the first number denotes Rowena's monetary payoff and the second number denotes Colin's monetary payoff.

There are two main ways to visualize such situations. For now, consider the matrix:[2]

$$\begin{array}{c|c} S & \boxed{0,2} \\ N & \boxed{1,0} \end{array}$$

Figure 4.1   Rowena's sacrifice situation

Here, we let each of Rowena's strategies be represented by a row in the matrix; maybe now you begin to understand why she is called Rowena? To press home the point, suppose

---

[1] In terms of our above notation, consequences are denoted $c = (c_R, c_C)$, where the subscripts denote Rowena and Colin respectively. That is, $c(S) = (0, 2)$ and $c(N) = (1, 0)$.

[2] If you are a mathematician, you might object to calling this figure a matrix. Since there are two numbers in each cell, it is technically a bi-matrix. I apologize, but sometimes it is better to relax terminology a little bit in order not to alienate non-mathematicians.

Colin can make a similar sacrifice for Rowena. Then, we draw Colin's matrix like this:

$$
\begin{array}{cc}
S & N \\
\hline
\multicolumn{1}{|c|}{2,0} & \multicolumn{1}{c|}{0,1} \\
\hline
\end{array}
$$

Figure 4.2   Colin's sacrifice situation

Rowena is the row player and Colin is the column player; this is easy to remember. Recall that we always list Rowena's payoff first.

Our next step is to visualize a bilateral sacrifice situation, where Rowena and Colin each simultaneously decide whether to make a sacrifice for the other. Putting the two matrices together yields the following illustration:

$$
\begin{array}{c|c|c|}
 & S & N \\
\hline
S & 2,2 & 0,3 \\
\hline
N & 3,0 & 1,1 \\
\hline
\end{array}
$$

Figure 4.3   A bilateral sacrifice situation (the social dilemma)

Suppose both Rowena and Colin are entirely selfish. In that case, and only in that case, we can use the monetary payoffs as utility functions.[3] That is, $U_i = c_i$. The bilateral sacrifice *situation* is also a bilateral sacrifice *game*. For future reference, allow me to include it as a figure, even if it looks identical to Figure 4.3, only now the numbers in the cells are *utils* instead of dollars:

$$
\begin{array}{c|c|c|}
 & S & N \\
\hline
S & 2,2 & 0,3 \\
\hline
N & 3,0 & 1,1 \\
\hline
\end{array}
$$

Figure 4.4   A bilateral sacrifice game (the social dilemma game)

By definition, each rational player in a game maximizes their own expected utility. So, what will Rowena and Colin do?

---

[3] Remember we have already decided to neglect risk aversion. Players are risk neutral in the terminology of Footnote 5 of Chapter 3.

The standard answer is that both Rowena and Colin will play N, and the standard argument is this: "No matter what Colin does, Rowena is better off if she plays N. Likewise, no matter what Rowena does, Colin is better off if he plays N." We shall accept that argument. No rational player makes a sacrifice in a social dilemma *game*. In other words, the outcome is always inefficient when rational players play a social dilemma game.

As will become clear, there are many situations that share the tension between individuals' interests and the group's interest. Social dilemmas can have more than two players and more than two strategies per player. But the 2 × 2 setting is the simplest, so I shall stick with it for the time being.[4]

If Rowena and Colin are not selfish, it is crucial to distinguish between the situation and the game. Therefore, please make sure you can answer this exercise.

Exercise 4.1 *Which of these two matrices defines a situation, and which defines a game?*

	S	N
S	$u_R(S,S), u_C(S,S)$	$u_R(S,N), u_C(S,N)$
N	$u_R(N,S), u_C(N,S)$	$u_R(N,N), u_C(N,N)$

Matrix 1

	S	N
S	$c_R(S,S), c_C(S,S)$	$c_R(S,N), c_C(S,N)$
N	$c_R(N,S), c_C(N,S)$	$c_R(N,N), c_C(N,N)$

Matrix 2

Figure 4.5   Situation or game?

---

[4] A famous early analysis of a 2 × 2 social dilemma used the framing of two prisoners who were taken in for questioning. They are interrogated in separate rooms. Each prisoner is told she will get a reduced sentence if she confesses, no matter what the other prisoner says. But if no prisoner confesses, they both get a more lenient sentence than if both confess. (Please check that this story fits the social dilemma payoff structure.) Therefore, the 2 × 2 social dilemma is often referred to as the Prisoners' Dilemma.

Magical Reasoning

Does utility maximization alone imply that selfish players will always play N in a social dilemma situation (equivalently, that a player must play N in a social dilemma *game*)? Well, not quite. Rowena might think that if she plays S, then Colin will also do so. If that is true, she might earn more by playing S. But can this belief be true? Rowena and Colin play simultaneously, so there is no way for Rowena's action to affect Colin's action. Thus, these beliefs are "magical" and not rational.[5] In reality, some people hold magical beliefs. They might hold selfish preferences, but they believe in some form of Karma. For example, they might think that if they fail to vote, then the turnout for their preferred candidate will be low. To avoid losing the election, they therefore vote.

According to the language of decision theory, these magical thinkers are irrational. Their behavior is inconsistent with the basic axioms of von Neumann and Morgenstern, as well as those of Savage. Yet, this form of irrationality can be socially beneficial, so perhaps it should be applauded and encouraged?

---

[5] If you are not convinced that magical beliefs are empirically wrong, think about what it would imply if they were correct. For example, if there are many magical thinkers in a social dilemma experiment, and they are right, we would see that one player playing S would raise the probability that the other player in the pair also plays S. For example, if there are two players, and s is the average frequency of S being played, then the proportion of (S, S) would be larger than s^2. Likewise, the proportion of (N, N) would be larger than $(1 - s)^2$. Cason, Sharma, and Vadovic (2020) show that even outside spectators, who do not themselves play, predict that players will be able to correlate their behavior in such a magical way (but unsurprisingly find no evidence the magic works).

Altruism

Consider next a case of unselfish players. For example, suppose both Rowena and Colin care about each other. Both have preferences that can be described by the utility function

$$U_i = c_i + \alpha c_j, \tag{4.1}$$

where $\alpha > 0$ and $j \neq i$. That is, Rowena's utility function is $U_R = c_R + \alpha c_C$ and Colin's utility function is $U_C = c_C + \alpha c_R$. (Since α does not have an index, Rowena and Colin care equally for each other.) What does the presence of altruism α imply for the game? Please check you understand how we arrive at the following game matrix:

	S	N
S	$2 + 2\alpha, 2 + 2\alpha$	$3\alpha, 3$
N	$3, 3\alpha$	$1 + \alpha, 1 + \alpha$

Figure 4.6   The Altruists' social dilemma game

Exercise 4.2 *Which strategy will Rowena play in the game in Figure 4.6?*

Does altruism vary much across countries? If so, could it help explaining the lost-wallet evidence we discussed in Chapter 2? In a recent survey of global preferences, altruism was measured as the fraction of an unexpected "windfall" gain that one would give to a good cause.[6] The authors of the lost-wallet experiment find that this form of altruism is *negatively* related to honest reporting of the wallet.[7] That is, countries where people report wanting to give a larger fraction of the

---

[6] The global preference survey is described in Falk et al. (2018). On altruism, the exact survey question was of the form: "Imagine the following situation: Today you unexpectedly received 1,000 Euro. How much of this amount would you donate to a good cause?"

[7] See Tannenbaum et al. (2023).

windfall are countries where a smaller fraction of the wallets are reported to the owner. It seems we must look elsewhere for an explanation to the lost-wallet evidence.[8]

Egalitarianism

Altruism is not the only sort of unselfishness. For example, some people dislike inequality.[9] In that case, hurting people who are ahead can be as desirable as helping people who are behind. Suppose now that both Rowena and Colin are somewhat egalitarian, in the sense that their preferences can be described by the utility function

$$U_i = c_i - \beta \left| c_i - c_j \right|, \qquad (4.2)$$

where $\beta > 0$ and $j \neq i$, and $\left| c_i - c_j \right|$ denotes the *absolute value* of the difference $c_i - c_j$. Since β does not have an index, both players care equally about inequality. Please check you understand how we arrive at the following game matrix:

	S	N
S	2, 2	$-3\beta, 3 - 3\beta$
N	$3 - 3\beta, -3\beta$	1, 1

Figure 4.7   The Egalitarians' social dilemma game

Exercise 4.3 *Which strategy will Rowena play in the game in Figure 4.7?*

---

[8] Perhaps we should not give up completely on the hypothesis that altruism has some positive role to play. There are other possible reasons for the poor correlation. For example, answers to hypothetical questions about generosity might not be informative about actual generosity.

[9] There are many aspects of inequality. Here, I refer to inequality of outcomes. People also care about inequality of opportunity, and they may care differently about inequality depending on the source – for example whether inequality is caused by external factors or by factors under people's control.

Here, the behavior of rational people depends on what they believe others are going to do. What is then a rational belief? Can we predict how people will behave under such circumstances? Clearly, if β is large enough, both Rowena and Colin would like to do the same as each other, and they would rather play (S, S) than (N, N).

Dutifulness and Norms

Sometimes, we act unselfishly simply because it is the right thing to do. For example, most of us have learned that stealing is wrong. Therefore, even if we could steal without fear of discovery or punishment, we would not do so.

For concreteness, think about the unmanned roadside stands with fruits and vegetables that can be found in many rural areas across the world. You can take as much as you like, and a price list specifies how much you should pay and how to pay it. Since nobody else is around, you could easily get away with not paying. Still, almost everyone pays.

Many situations are similarly governed by internalized social norms; some actions are permitted, other actions are forbidden.[10] An important role of morality as well as of laws is to define who is entitled to do what when.

Recall the general utility function (3.1). A simple way to represent preferences for rule compliance, for otherwise selfish people, is through the special case

$$u_i(s) = \begin{cases} c_i(s) - \lambda_i \mu & \text{if } s_i \text{ is forbidden;} \\ c_i(s) & \text{if } s_i \text{ is permitted,} \end{cases} \quad (4.3)$$

where μ is a parameter indicating how bad society considers it to be that this particular rule is violated. For example, not paying for the fruit you take from the farmer's roadside

---

[10] If only one action is permitted, we say this action is prescribed.

stand constitutes theft. Therefore, in many societies, the social condemnation μ would be large. To the extent that a customer internalizes laws and social norms, it is thus an easy decision to pay rather than to steal, even if stealing entails no risk of detection. (Note that ardent liberals typically approve of this internalized social pressure to preserve property rights.)

Now, suppose Rowena and Colin live in a society where the action N is forbidden. For example, they can both fish in a shared lake, and there is a rule saying that they should not fish this time of the year. However, it is impossible to monitor the fishing. They are both selfish, but share the loyalty (aversion to rule-breaking) λ. Then, their social dilemma game becomes:

	S	N
S	2,2	$0, 3 - \lambda\mu$
N	$3 - \lambda\mu, 0$	$1 - \lambda\mu, 1 - \lambda\mu$

Figure 4.8   The Norm-abiders' social dilemma game

Exercise 4.4 *What will Rowena do if the game is like Figure 4.8?*

Exercise 4.5 *Suppose now Rowena and Colin only feel bad about violating the norm to play S if the other player respects it. (i) What does the game look like then? (ii) What will Rowena do?*

Does dutifulness vary across countries? If so, might it explain the evidence from the lost-wallet experiment we discussed in Chapter 2? We return to this question in Chapter 5.

Social Esteem

Sometimes, an important motive for sacrificing is to impress others. You might want to send the message that you care, that you genuinely want to do your share, or that you take your duties seriously. This *signaling* motive always comes on top of some more basic motive. If people didn't differ in their altruism, fairness, or dutifulness, there would be nothing to signal. Still, it is quite possible that the signaling motive is decisive for the sacrifice.[11]

Clearly, such "virtue signaling" only makes sense if observers do not already know the actor's virtues. That is, signaling requires *asymmetric information*, which I introduce in Chapter 16.

Entitlements and Self-Serving Bias

Duties are constraining. Therefore, it is not too surprising that many people try to escape the moralizing of the "inner police." We tell ourselves there is no moral rule, or if there is one then it favors our side. Here is an experiment that illustrates the point:[12]

Two subjects are given several poker chips that can be exchanged for money. However, the exchange requires the two subjects to agree about how to share the chips. If they cannot agree, no subject gets any money. In Treatment 1, each chip is worth the same amount of money. In Treatment 2, the chips are worth twice as much in the hands of subject A than in the hands of Subject B. In both treatments, the subjects are free to discuss, but they are unable to meet up afterwards.

[11] For a detailed discussion of this point in the context of gift giving and helping, see Ellingsen and Johannesson (2011, Section 3.1).

[12] The original experiments were conducted by Alvin Roth in collaboration with various coauthors, and results are scattered across several articles published in the period 1979–1982. It would be desirable to have a large and focused replication study.

As you might have guessed, Treatment 1 poses no problem. Almost all subjects divide the chips equally. Treatment 2 is different. Subject B is likely to insist A gets 1/3 and B gets 2/3. Subject A often proposes that the chips are divided equally. Usually, both sides will apply to an equality norm, but one side focuses on equal number of chips, and the other focuses on an equal amount of money. When neither side is willing to budge, there is disagreement and the money is forgone.

Self-serving interpretations of entitlements are more likely to occur when situations are less transparent. One of my favorite experiments asks subjects to engage in a pre-trial bargaining task.[13] The task is based on a real court case. A motorcyclist has been hit by a car and sues for damages. In the real case, pre-trial bargaining failed and a judge made a ruling, but the experimental subjects only know the damages the motorcyclist sought. Subjects representing the motorcyclist get paid money in proportion to the damages obtained, and subjects representing the car driver get paid money in proportion to the damages resisted. There are two experimental treatments. Let me call them "subjective" and "objective." In the subjective treatment, subjects get allocated to their roles before they read the case material. In the objective treatment, they read the case material first.

Before bargaining, subjects make private guesses about the judge's decision. They also get to state privately what damages they find fair. In the subjective treatment, discrepancies are large: Subjects representing the motorcyclist not only think larger damages are fair, they also guess that the judge has awarded larger damages. In the objective treatment, discrepancies are much smaller. As a result, the rate of bargaining impasse is also considerably smaller in the objective treatment.

---

[13] The experiment was originally reported in Babcock, Issacharoff, Loewenstein, and Camerer (1995).

It seems likely that many strikes, wars, and other costly disagreements are ultimately caused by parties being unable to see the other side's point of view.[14]

Self-serving biases are well known from religious texts as well as from classic works of moral philosophy. According to David Hume, self-serving bias is one of the three main reasons why we need government, as people are unable to separate what is just and fair from what is in their own interest.[15] Likewise, in his classic book *The Theory of Moral Sentiments*, Adam Smith argues that distinct rules are useful because they counteract self-deception.[16] If society only provides general direction instead of clear rules, people tend to tell themselves their actions are moral even when they are not:

This self-deceit, this fatal weakness of mankind, is the source of half the disorders of human life. If we saw ourselves in the light that others see us, or in which they would see us if they knew all, a reformation would generally be unavoidable. We could not otherwise endure the sight.

(Smith, 1790, Part III, Ch. IV)

---

[14] Babcock and Loewenstein (1997) summarize several papers on self-serving bias, involving both the laboratory experiment referenced above and a field study of strikes among public school teachers in Pennsylvania. The field study shows that the strikes tended to follow negotiations where the employers and the teachers' union were both pointing to wages in "comparison districts" and where these comparison districts were more different from each other. That is, at least some of the comparison districts were chosen in a self-serving manner. On a grander scale, David Welch's book *Justice and the Genesis of War* from 1993 argues that conflicting interpretations of justice play a major role in many of the great wars.

[15] See Part I, Essay V: On the Origin of Government, in *Essays: Moral, Political and Literary*, originally published in 1742.

[16] The first edition is from 1759, and the sixth edition, much expanded, is from 1790. In between, Smith published *An Inquiry into the Causes and Nature of the Wealth of Nations* in 1776. The two books are closely linked and mutually consistent, with *Moral Sentiments* focusing more on individual motivation and *Wealth of Nations* focusing more on social structure.

Cooperation

Originally, the word cooperation meant "working together." British spelling emphasizes this meaning of the word: co-operation. When two people both make sacrifices in a social dilemma, that is a clear instance of cooperation; they work together toward a good outcome for both.

What if Rowena makes a sacrifice and Colin does not – does it make sense to say Rowena cooperates? I think it does not. Just as it takes two to tango, it takes (at least) two to cooperate. Rowena needs to cooperate *with somebody*; if Colin does not cooperate, how can Rowena cooperate *with* Colin?[17]

There is another reason not to equate beneficial sacrifice and cooperation: cooperation does not require sacrifice. Indeed, selfish people may be highly successful in working together. If their interests are aligned, why would they not cooperate? Rowing a large boat, hunting a large animal, lifting a heavy object: all of these are examples where a common goal can drive even the most egoistic group of people to cooperate smoothly. Two-person versions of these situations often have a material payoff structure similar to that in Figure 4.9:

	H	L
H	3,3	0,1
L	1,0	1,1

Figure 4.9   A coordination situation

Here, we may think of the action *H* as working hard, and the action *L* as working little. Suppose Rowena cares only about

---

[17] That said, you should be aware that many writers in social sciences as well as in biology define cooperation as individual sacrifice to benefit others. Changing such language conventions is difficult, however inappropriate they may be.

her own material payoff. Then, Rowena will indeed want to work hard if she thinks Colin is also likely to do so.

On the other hand, we would typically not call it cooperation if each player has a strategy that always yields the best consequences for her and that strategy just happens to also be beneficial for others. (For example, if we modify Figure 4.9 so that the strategy (H, L) yields payoff $(2, 1)$ and (L, H) yields $(1, 2)$ each player always gets the highest payoff by playing H, so (H, H) does not involve true cooperation.) We might summarize as follows.

Definition 1 (Cooperation) *A group engages in voluntary cooperation if each member of the group takes an action that benefits others (given what they do), even though that action is not certain to benefit oneself.*

Observe that it does not follow from this definition that cooperation is always desirable. If each member sacrifices more than other members gain, the group is better off by not cooperating.

Food for Thought 4.1 *In the 2018 Swedish parliamentary election, more than 87 percent of eligible voters participated. Given the high level of participation, there is only a tiny probability that any individual vote affects the outcome of the election. (i) Why do Swedes vote to such a large extent, do you think? (ii) Several countries now allow voting through the internet. What are the pros and cons of this option in view of your answer under (i)?*

5

Shared Understandings
and Values

So far, we have taken the situation for granted. In fact, we have implicitly assumed that everyone perfectly understands who the relevant players are, what they can do, and what the relevant consequences are. Everyone is dividing reality into distinct episodes and they do so in the same way. But where do these individual understandings and preferences come from, and how do understandings become shared? To discuss these questions, we need some more concepts.

The group and the individual

Figure 5.1 outlines the relationship between our key concepts.

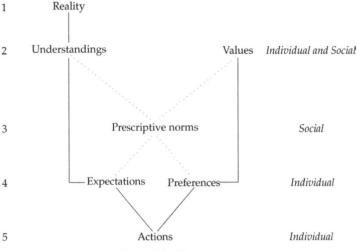

Figure 5.1 Key concepts

Let us first briefly introduce each of the five levels. Starting at level 1, define *reality* as everything that has happened, everything that could have happened, and everything that could happen in the future. Even if we confine ourselves to the small part of reality that concerns actions that people take and their consequences, reality is extremely rich, and our understanding of it necessarily remains limited.

At level 2 are individuals' shared understanding of reality as well as their shared values. The shared understanding might be thought of as those strategies and associated outcomes that people (in the relevant society) pay attention to. The values express how society rates these strategies and outcomes; this is the function v in Equation 3.1. When we discuss *the game that people play*, we are thus considering the second level.

At level 3 are those strategies that the society recommends on the basis of its shared understandings and values.

At level 4 are the expectations that various individuals hold about how others will act. The dividing line between understandings and beliefs is analytically clear. Understandings concern what the situation is, while beliefs concern what others are going to do in the situation. However, when we study the actions people take, we normally observe neither understandings nor beliefs. Hence, it can be difficult to distinguish them. Let me give an example. In his comparison of Genovese traders and Maghribi traders during the late medieval period, Greif (1994) argues that the Maghribi traders tended to keep close tabs on each other, and that if an employee had ever cheated, that employee would subsequently be shunned by everyone. By contrast, the Genovese society would pay less attention to potential employees' past misdemeanors in other relationships. Since Maghribi employees stood to lose more from cheating, pay did not need to be as high. Did the Genovese employers actually think about potential employees' long history, but neglected it because they thought other employers would also neglect it? Or did they not even consider a person's long history? In the first case, the difference between the two societies is located at level 4 (beliefs), in the second case, it is located at level 2 (understandings). Yet, the difference in pay is the same regardless.[1]

We devote Chapter 6 to analyzing expectations; this is where the power of game theory is essential. Level 4 is also where we find the preferences, i.e., the utility function u_i of Equation 3.1 for everyone who is considered to be part of the situation. We already discussed how social values may enter the preferences. In Chapter 8 we further extend our analysis of preferences.

Finally, at level 5 are the actions that everyone takes on the basis of their preferences and expectations.

Let me now address levels 2 and 3 in more detail.

---

[1] You may want to return to this example after you have read the next chapter, which formally introduces equilibrium analysis, and Chapter 11 which introduces long-run relationships.

Understanding Natural Reality

How do consequences depend on behavior? That is, how does the world work? Societies differ in their approaches to understanding the natural world. Some societies leave the interpretation of reality to shamans, priests, or other authority figures. But much of the world now leaves this task to science, with its more open and open-ended process for determining which understandings of reality are more correct.

Natural science builds our understanding of what is physically feasible. Often, natural science is complementary to folk wisdom. For example, early in history farmers learned that their harvests would be bigger if they treated the soil with manure. During the 20th century, scientific understanding of the underlying chemical processes enabled large-scale production of artificial fertilizer, revolutionizing farming.[2]

The modern approach to science can be traced back at least to the work of Francis Bacon, whose book *The New Organon* was published in 1620. Bacon scolded earlier thinkers for jumping too fast from isolated observations based on convenient measurements to general theories, which they then tended to believe with excessive certainty. Bacon advocated a more gradual building of theory, with greater emphasis on experiments and greater readiness to question and revise basic assumptions considering the new evidence. Bacon was convinced that this method would furnish a better

---

[2] Being Norwegian, it is part of my heritage to be proud of the contributions to agriculture by Kristian Birkeland and Samuel Eyde, who in 1903 devised a process for extracting nitrogen from air. The project itself was all due to Eyde, who was an engineer and an entrepreneur, but the key invention was due to the physicist Birkeland. Eyde founded two of Norway's greatest ever companies, Elkem and Norsk Hydro, and was motivated by business success. Birkeland's main motive was to earn some money for his research into polar lights and solar winds. Highly controversial during Birkeland's lifetime (he died in 1917), his theory of the aurora was essentially proven correct in 1967, by data from a space probe.

understanding of nature, and that this understanding would be a source of great technological improvements.

Understanding Social Reality

People have wills and hypotheses of their own. They are also aware that other people have wills and hypotheses. Thus, as we have already discussed, individuals' behavior might depend on how they expect others to behave. For example, if a person thinks nobody else will be playing along with social reform or an organizational change, then the person herself may decide not to play along.

Thus, social science faces an additional challenge, over and above all the challenges that natural sciences such as Physics and Chemistry face. Physicists do not need to consider the atom's understanding of the world, just as chemists don't need to consider the deliberations of the molecule. By contrast, social scientists who neglect the understandings of individuals, and the extent to which these understandings are shared within the society, have little chance of understanding that society.

The fact that people can hold shared understandings is a challenge for our analysis, but offers great opportunity for societies, as we shall now see.

Culture and Institutions

Societies function because people have found ways to coordinate their understandings. We effortlessly agree with other people where and when to meet, and we can do so because we have found shared ways to represent geography and time. We can organize sports teams, choirs, and chess clubs, as well as huge industrial enterprises and whole countries. All this organization is possible because of our ability to build shared representations of reality rather than because we as individuals understand reality so well.

Societies are characterized not only by how they represent reality, but also by how they evaluate consequences. For example, as the name indicates, the World Values Survey (WVS) categorizes countries according to commonly held values. According to WVS, one important dimension is traditionalism versus secularism. Another is survival (roughly, collectivism) vs self-expression (roughly, individualism). WVS finds that traditionalistic and survival-oriented cultures are clustered in African and Islamic countries, whereas Protestant European countries are secular and individualistic. The United States is an example of a relatively traditionalistic yet highly individualistic country, whereas South Korea is an example of a relatively collectivistic yet highly secular country.

A reasonable definition of *culture* is the shared understandings and values of the relevant group. I adopt that definition here.[3]

At level 3, we return to the concept of prescriptive norms. Prescriptive norms specify what is forbidden and what is permitted.[4] What is forbidden in one situation may be permitted in another. For example, some cultures prohibit sex before marriage but permit it afterwards. Such conditional norms require that there is already a shared understanding of situations, for example regarding whether two individuals can be considered married or not. Both the nature and the tightness of prescriptive norms are affected by society's values.

---

[3] There are many other definitions of culture, and they are often wider. I agree with Harrison and Huntington (1980) that relatively narrow definitions are preferable for analytical purposes. My definition is even narrower than theirs, which is: "values, attitudes, beliefs, orientations, and underlying assumptions prevalent among people in a society."

[4] Occasionally, the literature on social norms defines a norm more narrowly as prescribed behavior, i.e., the correct behavior. I think the more general definition is more useful for our purposes here.

Sometimes prescriptive norms are called injunctive norms, and sometimes simply norms. However, the latter usage can be confusing, since the word norms is also often used to describe descriptive norms – what people tend to do (in morally laden situations), rather than what they are supposed to do. Some sociologists prefer to use the word mores instead of descriptive norms.

For example, collectivistic societies typically prescribe that the individual respect the interest of the family and also tend to regulate individuals' behavior more overall.

Here, I think about prescriptive norms broadly as *the rules for how people are supposed to relate to each other.*[5] That is, I use the concept of prescriptive norms in roughly the same way as many authors define *institutions.* To avoid confusion, let me from now on use the word "institutions" to denote prescriptive norms.[6]

All rules are recipes. They state what people are permitted to do and what they are forbidden from doing, not necessarily what they choose to do. Institutions can therefore be classified along two main dimensions. They can be *formal* or *informal,* and they can be *strong* or *weak.*

A formal institution is coded in a particular way – for example it may be written in a public document. Since the formal institutions are usually given names, they are sometimes called *nominal* and since they are often parts of law, they are sometimes called *legal* or *de jure.* Informal institutions are not explicitly codified. Figure 5.2 lists some formal and informal institutions:

---

[5] There are other kinds of rules. For example, people may have personal rules for how they lead their lives. Also, all societies have folkways, i.e., ways of furnishing the home, preparing food, tending to animals, and so on, which are not linked to externalities. These folkways, we do not call prescriptive norms.

[6] Many authors use the word institutions to denote the organizations that implement rules rather than the rules themselves. For example, they will use the word institution to denote governments, government agencies, voluntary associations, and even corporations. That is a defensible choice. Unfortunately, many of them also use the word to denote rules. Such elastic use of language, while sometimes rhetorically useful, inhibits clear thinking.

Formal/Legal institutions	Informal/Cultural institutions
Laws	*Conventions*
Regulations	*Customs*
Corporate charters	*Taboos*
Explicit contracts	*Implicit contracts*

Figure 5.2   Formal and informal institutions (prescriptive norms)

Institutions do not necessarily affect behavior. Some laws become irrelevant; it is still forbidden to enter the United Kingdom's Houses of Parliament wearing a suit of armor. Other laws become inappropriate; for example, in 1615 the Icelandic district of Westfjords formulated a decree to kill on sight any Basque person caught in the area.[7] When the decree was finally repealed in 2015, it had not been taken seriously for a long time. Rules that are obeyed are called *strong* institutions; rules that are ignored are called *weak* institutions. Strong institutions are sometimes called *real* or *de facto*, mostly to make the rhetorical point that an informal institution can be stronger than a formal (i.e., *nominal, de jure*) institution that applies to the same situation; I do this in Chapter 10 when discussing how nominal authority does not ensure real authority.

Sometimes, the breaking of formal rules is quite consensual, as with the inappropriate laws the legislators have not yet come around to repeal; the decision not to kill Basques in the Westfjords is a case in point. At other times, the replacing of formal institutions by informal institutions is conflictual. For example, in autocratic societies, the Leader (Emperor, King, President, Party Chairman) will often be able to act in contradiction to the law, against the wish of parliaments, courts, or other bodies holding the formal power.

---

[7] I am grateful to Joakim Semb for this example.

We may also distinguish rules that are enforced through external punishments or rewards and rules that are enforced through internalized social pressure. Until now, we have only considered internalized norms. From Chapter 11 onwards, we shall study external enforcement in some detail.

Let me end the chapter with some examples of how and why culture is important.

Example 1: Culture, lost wallets, and economic success

Recall the lost-wallet experiment from Chapter 2. Why are people in some countries so much more willing to return the wallet than people in other countries are? To study this question, Tannenbaum et al. (2023) consider information from a variety of international surveys concerning people's morality.

A factor that stands out is called *generalized morality* and is obtained from the World Values Survey. It indicates whether "tolerance and respect for other people" is one of the top five qualities children are encouraged to learn at home (from a list of ten possible qualities such as obedience, hard work, or feelings of responsibility). A somewhat similar factor, taken from the so-called Moral Foundations Questionnaire, is defined as the weight that respondents place on fairness and individual rights relative to the weight they place on in-group loyalty and respect for established hierarchies.[8]

Generalized morality is not only closely related to unselfish behavior with respect to lost wallets. It is also closely related to overall economic prosperity, suggesting that morality is a foundation for material success. However, how do we know that it is the morality that drives prosperity and not the other

[8] The correlations are remarkably large; the correlation coefficient between the reporting rate and generalized morality is about 0.6. In fact, generalized morality is as closely related to observed wallet reporting rates as are the answers to a survey question (in a large Gallup poll) concerning how likely it is that a stranger living in this place would return a small lost item to its owner.

way around? Perhaps rich societies grow more tolerant? After all, as people get richer, they can better afford to behave morally.

To address this question, we need to study how morality has been shaped. One idea is that ancient historical circumstances have prompted some societies to be more kinship-oriented than other societies, either because it was beneficial for the individuals involved or because powerful political interests did not prevent it. Societies with a less kinship-oriented morality supported greater trust between strangers, which in turn benefited cooperation around new and large ventures. Such trust among strangers might not have been particularly valuable in a stable and stagnant world. However, the ability to trust non-kin would be essential for the more fluid connections required by the Industrial Revolution (see Example 3 below) and the path that followed. Recent research supports this idea; see relevant references in Chapter 20.

Example 2: Cultural change in Japan

Historian David Landes is the author of an essay entitled "Culture Makes Almost All the Difference." As an illustration of his thesis, Landes describes how Japan transformed its culture during the second half of the 19th century. The episode is known as the Meiji Restoration. It started with a revolt against the system of military dictatorship (feudal shogunate) that had lasted for about 250 years. At the center of the reforms was a reorientation of people's understandings and values:

> First came those tasks ordinary to government: a postal service, a new time standard, public education (for boys and then for girls as well), universal military service. General schooling diffused knowledge: that is what schools are for. But it also instilled discipline, obedience, punctuality, and a worshipful respect for the emperor. This was

the key to the development of a we/they national identity transcending the parochial loyalties nurtured by the feudal shogunate. The army and navy completed the job. Beneath the sameness of the uniform and the discipline, universal military service wiped out distinctions of class and place.

(Landes, 2000, p. 9)

Note how the first part of the quote highlights shared understandings, whereas the last part highlights shared values, especially the duty to make sacrifices for the benefit of the entire nation rather than merely the own family or clan.

The Meiji Restoration is widely regarded as a critical juncture in Japan's modernization.

Example 3: The scientific revolution

As we have already discussed, Francis Bacon proposed a new scientific method. Economic historian Joel Mokyr (2016) argues that Bacon did something even more important. Together with a small community of like-minded scholars around the world, he created a whole new scientific culture. The other scholars shared Bacon's view that reproducible experiments were the key to fundamental knowledge, but they also helped to build a community where the lessons from these experiments were jointly worked out and widely shared. Core values of this academic culture were openness, collaboration, and disclosure. The scientists were tolerant of opposing views and they would freely share their findings.

Of course, some of these values had been present long before. For example, Cicero (44 BCE) considered the duty to preserve and develop the truth to be the most important of all duties, and in principle this idea had been endorsed by Christianity well before Bacon. In practice, however, Christianity did not always support the search for truth, partly because it was sometimes difficult to draw the line between natural science and religion. The classical example of Christian ambivalence is the struggles of Catholics and Protestants alike with the (heliocentric) teachings of astronomers Copernicus and Galilei during the 16th and 17th centuries.

Mokyr's thesis is that the scientific revolution enabled the industrial revolution that took off more than a century later. More importantly, he claims that the scientific insights themselves would not have been produced and disseminated were it not for the academic culture and institutions that a group of European scientists established in the 17th and 18th centuries.[9]

Food for Thought 5.1 *Can you think about additional cases where political leaders – or people who want to become political leaders – have managed to change the culture in such a way as to make their society more prosperous? Can you also think about cases in which the leaders have changed culture in a way that made people poorer?*

Food for Thought 5.2 *During the Covid-19 pandemic, there were strong appeals to everyone to reduce their physical interaction with other people. Sometimes, these appeals were framed in terms of empathy: We should engage in social distancing because we care about others. Sometimes, they were framed in terms of obligations: We all have a responsibility to do what we can to make sure others do not fall ill. Which framing do you think was most effective, and why?*

Food for Thought 5.3 *A recent study reports that soccer matches have large impact on political attitudes in sub-Saharan Africa. Individuals surveyed in the days after an important victory for their national team are 37 percent less likely to identify with their ethnic group and 30 percent more likely to trust other ethnicities than individuals interviewed just before*

---

[9] This thesis is bold. Among other things, it invites a careful analysis of why a similar scientific revolution did not occur earlier and in other places. In earlier times, both China and many parts of the Muslim world were technologically more advanced than Europe. Mokyr's book addresses this question too.

these matches. There is also evidence of reduced civil conflict following soccer successes. Why can such seemingly irrelevant events affect the trust between people from different ethnicities? (Which are the parts of Figure 5.1 that you think are involved?)

6

Predicting Behavior in Games

After this grand overview, let us proceed with formalization.

We start at the bottom of Figure 5.1, i.e., with individual behavior. How can we predict actions when we know preferences? The answer is simple when only one person makes a choice, at least if the person is rational. The rational person will take an action that maximizes expected utility. But if several people take actions, the problem is more intricate. We need game theory.

Suppose an interaction can be properly described as a multi-player game and that all players can be described as rational. Sometimes, knowing the players' utility functions is all we need to predict behavior in the game. For example, if each player has a strategy that always yields higher utility than the player's other strategies regardless of what opponents do, we can safely predict that each player will play this so-called *strictly dominant strategy*.

You probably agree that the concept of a strictly dominant strategy is so simple it is unnecessary to define it formally. But I do so anyway. Why? Because I can then introduce the little bit of formal notation I need below in order to explain Nash equilibrium. Let a *strategy profile* $s = (s_1, ..., s_n)$ comprise one (possibly random) strategy per player and let s_{-i} denote the strategy profile of player i's opponents.[1] We can then define strictly dominant and strictly dominated strategies as follows:

Definition 2 *Player i's strategy s_i^+ is a strictly dominant strategy if $u_i(s_i^+, s_{-i}) > u_i(s_i, s_{-i})$ for all s_{-i} and all $s_i \neq s_i^+$.*

Definition 3 *Player i's strategy s_i^- is a strictly dominated strategy if $u_i(s_i^-, s_{-i}) < u_i(s_i, s_{-i})$ for all s_{-1} and some $s_i \neq s_i^-$.*

Likewise, we can define weakly dominant and weakly dominated strategies by replacing the strict inequalities by weak inequalities.

For example, in the Prisoners' Dilemma situation, sufficiently altruistic players will always play S whereas sufficiently selfish players will always play N. In other words, for the rational altruist, S is strictly dominant and N is strictly dominated. For the rational egoist, N is dominant and S is dominated.[2]

But, as we have already seen, many games lack both dominant and dominated strategies. Then, a player's best strategy depends on the player's beliefs. In order to predict what a player will do, we therefore need *a theory of what beliefs the player will arrive at.*

The most common theory is that players will tend to arrive at *correct* beliefs. Wait a minute, you might say! How can we be sure this is even possible? We have already assumed each player will take the best action she can, given the beliefs she holds. Now we are also assuming that all players hold correct beliefs – can we be sure it is logically possible for all

---

[1] The mathematician might object that we should introduce a separate symbol for mixed strategies, rather than pretending that s_i can be both a single object and a probability distribution over objects. I apologize for the abuse of notation.

[2] The qualifier "rational" is important. Recall that a selfish player may play S if the player holds the magical belief that the opponent is more likely to play S if she plays S.

the players both to maximize their expected utility and hold correct beliefs?

The answer is yes, it is logically possible. More precisely, any game in which each player has access to finitely many strategies has such a solution.[3] The formulation and proof of this result is due to the mathematician John Nash.[4] In his honor, the solution concept is known as *Nash equilibrium*.

In plain words, a Nash equilibrium is a (possibly random) strategy for each player such that no single player could be better off by changing her strategy: *Everyone plays a best response to the strategies of everyone else.* More formally, a Nash equilibrium is defined as follows.

Definition 4 *A strategy profile s^* is a Nash equilibrium if $u_i(s_i^*, s_{-1}^*) \geq u_i(s_i, s_{-1}^*)$ for all players i and strategies s_i.*

The careful reader will have noticed the definition says nothing explicitly about the players' beliefs. However, it is obvious that if all players correctly forecast what the opponent is going to do, no player can do better than by playing a best response to those beliefs. Thus, correct beliefs together with utility maximization are sufficient conditions for Nash equilibrium.[5]

When we are making predictions, it is good to know a solution will always exist. But what if there are many solutions? As we shall see, even simple games can have several Nash equilibria. This is not a weakness of the theory. Rather, it helps

---

[3] If players can choose from infinitely many strategies, we need some additional assumptions about the game's payoffs to be certain a solution exists.

[4] Since it relies on powerful existing theorems, the proof takes up only a single page. John Nash has proved other results that are mathematically more advanced, but this result from his doctoral dissertation in 1950 laid the foundation for modern game theory. The book and Hollywood film *A Beautiful Mind* is based on Nash's life and work. If you only have time for one, I recommend the book.

[5] There are many games in which players will be playing Nash equilibrium even if they have somewhat incorrect beliefs. That is, rational expectations are not always necessary for Nash equilibrium.

us to understand why two societies that have both similar technological opportunities and similar understandings and values (i.e., play the same game) can nonetheless end up with totally different behavior and consequences. It also invites the question: What determines the selection among equilibria? I provide some answers in Chapters 9 and 10.

Finding Nash Equilibria

In simple games, it is easy to find the Nash equilibria – at least to find those solutions that do not involve randomization. We call those solutions *pure strategy Nash equilibria.*

For example, consider the following coordination game (since we call it a game, you know the numbers are utilities, whose expectation the players maximize):

	H	L
H	3,3	0,1
L	1,0	1,1

Figure 6.1   A common-interest coordination game

Note that each equilibrium in a two-player game is a *pair of strategies* (a strategy profile), not a single strategy or a pair of utilities.

Exercise 6.1 *Which pure strategy Nash equilibria do you find in Figure 6.1?*

Now, try one more game, called the Distribution game.[6] (Note that we also relabel the strategies; now Rowena plays Top or Bottom and Colin plays Left or Right.)

---

[6] The literature sometimes refers to this game as the Battle of the Sexes. As the question is whether Rowena or Colin will get their way, that would be a natural label here as well. However, I prefer not to tell the gender stereotypical story of the game, which is that Colin wants to watch soccer and Rowena wants to watch opera.

	L	R
T	0,0	1,3
B	3,1	0,0

Figure 6.2   The Distribution game

The Distribution game belongs to a class of games called mixed-motive games, because the players agree that two consequences should be avoided, but they disagree about which of the remaining two consequences is preferable.

Exercise 6.2 *Which pure strategy Nash equilibria do you find in Figure 6.2?*

We shall not be much concerned about randomization – mixed strategies – in this book. For completeness, let me nonetheless give the following example:

	L	R
T	1, −1	−1, 1
B	−1, 1	1, −1

Figure 6.3   An Anti-coordination game

As you may easily check, this game has no equilibrium in pure strategies.[7] The only equilibrium entails each player randomizing, with equal probabilities, between both the pure strategies.[8]

---

[7] You may recognize this game as matching pennies: Rowena wins if both players choose the same face of the coin, and Colin wins if they show different faces. Another simple game that only has a mixed strategy equilibrium is stone-paper-scissors. Similar payoff structures appear in several sports. For example, penalty-taking in soccer has the characteristic that the shooter wants the ball to go where the goal-keeper is not, whereas the goal-keeper wants to be where the ball goes. Being unpredictable can similarly be important in many situations in business, policing, and politics. However, as this book is primarily about cooperation, I refrain from discussing these applications in any detail.

[8] If you want to compute the mixed strategy equilibrium, the key thing to note is that a rational player who is unpredictable must be indifferent between

Interpreting Nash Equilibria

Even when a game has a unique Nash equilibrium, the equilibrium does not always provide good predictions of how people will play. One reason is that the game may be too complex for players to "see through" it. Another reason is that players don't trust other players to think deeply enough.

In class, I like to illustrate these ideas by playing the Guessing game. It runs as follows. Each student picks an integer from 0 to 100. The student who picks the number closest to two-thirds of the median number wins 2 dollars If there are several winners, there is a playoff. In order not to ruin the fun associated with the classroom experiment, I won't write more about it here. (Check out Nagel, Büren, and Frank, 2017, if you want to know the intriguing history of the game.)

But let me show you the following game:

	A	B	C
A	20, 20	−100, −100	8, 16
B	−100, −100	8, 16	16, 12
C	16, 16	12, 12	12, 12

Figure 6.4   A high-risk game

If you were Rowena, what would you do? Can you find a Nash equilibrium in pure strategies?[9]

---

all the pure strategies she might be playing. Thus, we ask ourselves: what is the probability p_L, with which Colin plays L, that makes Rowena indifferent between T and B? That probability must solve the equation $p_L \times 1 + (1 - p_L) \times (-1) = p_L \times (-1) + (1 - p_L) \times 1$. The left-hand side of the equation is Rowena's payoff if she plays T and the right-hand side is the payoff if she plays B. A simple computation shows the only solution is $p_L = 1/2$.

[9] A few years ago, we ran an experiment where subjects played this game once. On that occasion, 45 percent of the subjects played the unique Nash equilibrium strategy A, and the remaining 55 percent played C. No subject played action B.

As people gather experience with a game, either from participating themselves or watching others, play usually converges to a Nash equilibrium eventually. In games that have several equilibria in pure strategies, such as the Distribution game, play will typically start out far away from any of these equilibria, and then converge to one of them over time as players gain experience. Sometimes, it is impossible to predict which equilibrium will emerge, even when we can predict with great confidence one of them will.

Multi-Stage Games

Social interactions often take place over time. Once we take dynamics into account, it becomes important to distinguish a player's strategy from what a player does at a given point in time. *A strategy is a complete plan.* That is, a player's strategy specifies what the player intends to do in every contingency.

Sometimes, multi-stage interactions are merely a sequence of single-stage interactions. For example, Rowena's opportunity to sacrifice for Colin might occur earlier than Colin's opportunity to sacrifice for Rowena. Then, we might represent the actions of the whole game as follows:

Figure 6.5   A Sequential Sacrifice game

Suppose Colin thinks about what Rowena did when he chooses his own action, and suppose Rowena anticipated that Colin would do so. How would you represent this game in a single payoff matrix? Ask yourself: (i) How many strategies does Rowena have? (ii) How many strategies does Colin have? Please think carefully before reading on.

I am sure you have counted Rowena's (pure) strategies correctly. They are two, S and N, just as before. But how many strategies does Colin have? You might think Colin also has two strategies. But because a strategy is a complete plan, Colin must decide what to do after each of Rowena's actions. Therefore, Colin has four strategies. Colin could choose to play S regardless of what Rowena has done; call this strategy SS. He could also play N regardless of what Rowena has done; call this strategy NN. Colin could also decide to play S if Rowena plays S and N if Rowena plays N; call this strategy SN. And he could do the reverse; call this strategy NS. (You may want to make a note next to this paragraph: "This is the place where the notation for conditional strategies is introduced!" We shall use it extensively.)

Please check that the game matrix may now be written:

	SS	SN	NS	NN
S	2,2	2,2	0,3	0,3
N	3,0	1,1	3,0	1,1

Figure 6.6 Sequential Sacrifice game in single matrix

Next, please check that this game has a unique Nash equilibrium (N, NN).

We usually cannot observe people's plans. The plan is in the planner's head.

What we can observe is the actions people take. In the equilibrium of the Sequential Sacrifice game, those actions are N for each player. We thus say (N, N) is the *Nash equilibrium outcome*. Sometimes, writers are sloppy and talk about equilibrium when they mean equilibrium outcome. When the two are not the same, that sloppiness can be confusing.

When moves are sequential, dominant strategy equilibrium tends to exist even more rarely than in related games with simultaneous moves. Intuitively, the reason is that later movers might in principle reward bad moves; if the first player does something silly, the second player does something silly too. The next exercise illustrates the point.

Exercise 6.3 *(i) Does any player have a dominant strategy in the Sequential Sacrifice game? (ii) Does any player have a dominated strategy?*

Payoff matrices describing sequential games soon become unwieldy, since the same numbers appear many times. That's one of the reasons why we often represent multi-stage games by trees instead. Below is a tree that describes the Sequential Sacrifice game.

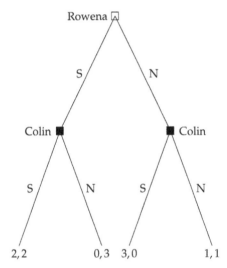

Figure 6.7 Sequential Sacrifice game as a tree

Another reason to use the tree format is that it is convenient for finding Nash equilibria. The tree can be pruned from the end. This so-called *backward induction* procedure runs as follows: (i) Cross out each branch that is dominated by another branch from the point of view of the last mover. In this example, cross out the two branches where Colin plays *S*. (ii) Given that these branches are crossed out, see whether the second-last mover wants to cross out any branch. In the example, we can cross out the branch where Rowena plays *S*. Again, we have arrived at the unique Nash equilibrium

(N, NN) (as well as a unique Nash equilibrium outcome (N, N)).[10]

An important insight, due to Reinhard Selten, is that there exists at least one such backward induction solution in all games that have a finite number of pure strategies at each stage. In fact, as will soon become clear, the backward induction procedure even does something more: It sometimes enables us to pick one Nash equilibrium over another. Those Nash equilibria that survive backward induction are called *subgame-perfect.*

A subgame is a part of the game that includes the last stage of the game and where players know what, if anything, has happened at earlier stages of the game. For example, in the Sequential Sacrifice game, the only subgame (apart from the whole game) is Stage 2. Stage 1 is not a subgame, as it fails to include the subsequent stage. *A subgame-perfect equilibrium is a Nash equilibrium of the entire game which also specifies Nash equilibrium play in each subgame.*

In the Sequential Sacrifice game, the only Nash equilibrium at Stage 2 is N, so it follows that the Nash equilibrium (N, NN) is also subgame-perfect. This conclusion is evident regardless of whether we look at Figure 6.5 or Figure 6.7.[11]

---

[10] Of course, it is at least as easy to find the subgame-perfect equilibrium outcome using backward induction in our original Figure 6.5. However, the trees are much better when early moves affect which moves are available later (see next footnote).

[11] You are entitled to ask: Why don't we simply represent dynamic games as in Figure 6.5? This seems to be the simplest figure, it allows backward induction, and it even preserves information about when the payoffs arise; that information is lost in both the other figures. The answer is that many games lack such a clean separation between stages. If the payoffs associated with Colin's strategies at Stage 2 depend on what Rowena did at Stage 1, more complicated figures are required.

Let us end by considering the following game tree:

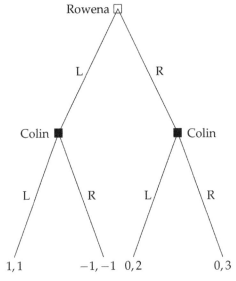

Figure 6.8   A Threatening game

Exercise 6.4 *(i) Does the Threatening game have a subgame-perfect equilibrium? (ii) Does it have any Nash equilibrium that is not subgame-perfect?*

The Threatening game illustrates the following scenario: Colin wants Rowena to play *R*. The only way he can hope to convince her to do so is to threaten to play *R* if Rowena plays *L*. But should Rowena believe this threat? No! She knows the best Colin can do if she plays *L* is to also play *L*. Subgame-perfect Nash equilibrium disallows threats that are not credible because they are too costly to carry out.

I hear you saying: "Wait. People often carry out threats. Colin may feel a need to preserve his reputation, or he may just feel bad about not carrying out what he has said he would do." I agree. But this problem cannot be addressed by modifying the solution concept. Instead, we need to modify the game. If reputation is important for future interactions, either those interactions should be part of the strategies we consider (we discuss ongoing relationships in Chapter 11), or the utility loss should be incorporated into the payoffs (a possibility that we discuss in Chapter 8).

7

A Model of Anarchy

We now have the concepts we need for describing the most primitive forms of society, or at least the most primitive society considered by the philosopher Thomas Hobbes, in his book *Leviathan* from 1651.[1] Hobbes famously imagines the terrors of life in the so-called state of nature:

> Whatsoever therefore is consequent to a time of Warre, where every man is Enemy to every man; the same is consequent to the time, wherein men live without other security, than what their own strength, and their own invention shall furnish them withall. In such condition there is no place for industry, because the fruit thereof is uncertain, and consequently no culture of the earth, no navigation nor the use of commodities that may be imported by sea, no commodious building, no instruments of moving and removing such things as require much force, no knowledge of the face of the earth, no account of time, no arts, no letters, no society, and which is worst of all, continual fear

---

[1] Old classics are available to read for free on the internet. At the time of writing, I was using this link: http://files.libertyfund.org/files/869/0161_Bk.pdf.

and danger of violent death, and the life of man, solitary, poor, nasty, brutish, and short.

(Part I, Ch. 13, Para. 9)

Let me use a simple model to illustrate Hobbes' logic.[2] Suppose there are two persons. Each person has access to a separate plot of land and the labor of their own body. Suppose labor can be divided up in any way between two tasks, making food and making weapons. Normalize the time each person has available to 1. Denote person i's food production by x_i and denote the weapons production

$$y_i = 1 - x_i. \tag{7.1}$$

Denote the total food production $x = x_1 + x_2$ and the total weapons production $y = y_1 + y_2$.

We ignore leisure. We have already assumed players are risk neutral. Moreover, we assume the persons are selfish and get utility from their own food consumption only; they do not get joy from watching their weapons. Thus, we can write i's utility function

$$U_i = c_i. \tag{7.2}$$

We shall assume that everything that is produced will be consumed. Therefore:

$$c_1 + c_2 = x. \tag{7.3}$$

Before moving on, let us check I am being clear enough.

Exercise 7.1 *(i) How much food is produced if each person spends all his time producing food? (ii) How much food is produced if each person spends sixty percent of the time*

---

[2] You might think this is too simple. If so, please recall Footnote 8 of Chapter 3.

producing food? (iii) Which combinations of utility are technically achievable?

Figure 7.1 represents the production possibilities and the consumption possibilities graphically. To the left, the figure denotes the combinations of food and weapons that may be produced. To the right are the combinations of utility that may be attained. The north-east frontier shows the maximal attainable utilities. These are the *efficient outcomes* or the *resource constraint.*[3]

How are goods allocated in an anarchy? According to Hobbes, people have "no security other than their own strength," so let us simply assume whoever has the most weapons will get all the available food. Intuitively, what do you think will happen? How much food will be produced?

Let us use game theory to think through the problem. A person's strategy is the combination of food and the weapons the person decides on. For simplicity, we can think of person *i*'s strategy merely as the weapons production, y_i, since that

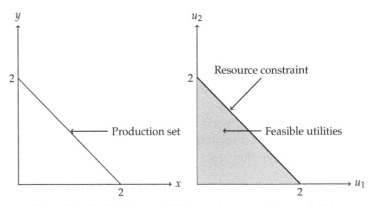

Figure 7.1 Production possibilities and consumption possibilities

---

[3] They are sometimes called the *Pareto-frontier*. Recall from Chapter 3 that Vilfredo Pareto defined an efficient outcome as an outcome such that no person can be made better off without another person being made worse off.

also decides the food production $x_i = 1 - y_i$. A person's utility expressed as a function of the strategies, $u_i(y_i,y_j) = c_i(y_i,y_j)$, is thus

$$u_i = \begin{cases} x & \text{if } y_i > y_j; \\ x/2 & \text{if } y_i = y_j; \\ 0 & \text{if } y_i < y_j. \end{cases}$$

Can you find any Nash equilibria in this game?[4] It is simpler to analyze than you think. Begin by asking yourself: Could there be any equilibrium in which $y_i < y_j$? When you have understood why the answer is no, ask yourself: Could there be any equilibrium in which $y_1 = y_2 = y < 1$? Again, you will see the answer is no. Finally, ask yourself: Is it an equilibrium to have $y_1 = y_2 = 1$? The answer is yes. This is the only Nash equilibrium! In other words, the model predicts that the two persons end up with the worst possible consequences, with all resources being used to produce weapons. We conclude this game is a social dilemma: when each party pursues the own interest, the collective consequences are the worst imaginable.

This model is silent on whether there is fighting or merely investing in weapons. In this sense it illustrates that failure to cooperate can be every bit as bad as active conflict.

Of course, this model is not entirely realistic. For there to exist people in the first place, they must have had some food to consume. But the point of a model is never to be maximally realistic. A map of the world in proportions 1:1 is not a useful map.[5] The virtue of a formal model is that it highlights some important insight that does not disappear as we make the

[4] This game has infinitely many pure strategies, so Nash's theorem does not guarantee any equilibrium exists.

[5] Here are two famous and funny expositions of the pointlessness of large maps. Lewis Carroll, in *Sylvie and Bruno Concluded*, Ch. XI, 1895, lets a dialogue about the 1:1 map finish with the exchange:

"Have you used it much?" I enquired.

"It has never been spread out, yet," said Mein Herr: "the farmers objected: they said it would cover the whole country, and shut out the sunlight! So

model more realistic. Here, that insight is the tension between personal interest and group interest.

Exiting Anarchy

The basic question that occupied Hobbes is: How do societies exit from this anarchical state?

Leviathan was written during the English Civil War (1642–1651), which originated in the Parliament's objection to King Charles' increasingly tyrannical behavior, including the imposition of new taxes without Parliamentary consent. Hobbes argued that a strong ruler – preferably a sovereign monarch – was needed to avoid the war of all against all. The ruler will protect people against each other by (credibly) threatening to punish thieves and thugs.

Hobbes is sometimes seen as the Enlightenment's first "contractarian" thinker, as he argued that the ruler's power is in the interest of the subordinates and thus could have been granted by them. This justification is markedly different from the historically popular justification that the King's authority is granted by God.[6]

Throughout history, there have been extensive debates about Hobbes' analysis. One criticism is that Hobbes exaggerates

---

we now use the country itself, as its own map, and I assure you it does nearly as well."

In 1946, Jorge Luis Borges wrote a one-paragraph short-story called "On Exactitude in Science." The Wikipedia entry (https://en.wikipedia.org/wiki/On_Exactitude_in_Science) is longer than the story itself. The story would probably satisfy Antoine de Saint-Exupéry (see Footnote 8 of Chapter 3).

[6] *Leviathan* was published after Charles I had been beheaded at the Parliament's order in 1649 and just as his son and successor Charles II was dethroned. As Hobbes was making his own analysis of the Civil War in *Behemoth* (written in 1668 and published in 1681), Britain remained on the road to becoming a parliamentary democracy. That road started with the Magna Carta in 1215. After the bumpiness produced by the tyrannical reign of Charles I, and the brief flirtation with Republicanism under Oliver Cromwell (1653–1658), democratization continued with the Bill of Rights in 1689 and the Act of Settlement 1701.

human selfishness. We have already studied how, in principle, compassion and duty may suffice to sustain cooperation.
However, I don't think anyone truly believes that compassion
and duty can always suffice to sustain desirable cooperation,
so Hobbes' concerns remain valid.

The most famous criticisms of Hobbes' thesis are those
of Jean-Jacques Rousseau. In his *Discourse on Inequality*
(1755), Rousseau makes two objections. The first is related
to the point that human nature is not as grim as Hobbes por-
trayed it.[7] A great deal of cooperation can be achieved due to
feelings of compassion and duty. According to Rousseau, it
is civilization with its emphasis on hierarchy and pride that
poisons peoples' minds and prevents the peaceful coexistence
often found among the "savages" – whose lives are therefore
preferable.

Rousseau's second objection, laid out in greater detail in
The Social Contract from 1762, is this: Uncontested powers
in the hands of a sovereign ruler are likely to benefit the few at
the expense of the many. Rather than relying on a sovereign
ruler, we need to establish a social contract that binds everyone, including the authority figures themselves. Rulers should
also be subject to rules.

Similar concerns about rulers' abuse of power had been
expressed already by John Locke, in *Two Treatises of
Government*. The book was first published anonymously in
1689, but it made little immediate impact. It slowly gained
prominence and influence and, from 1750 onwards, it was
being used as a starting point for some of the most important debates of the day. It inspired not only Rousseau, but
also Thomas Jefferson, Alexander Hamilton, and James
Madison. In 1776, Jefferson included whole sentences from
Two Treatises in the *Declaration of Independence*. The only

---

[7] An earlier version of this critique is due to Joseph Butler, an English bishop
and philosopher active in the first part of the 18th century. Butler influenced
both David Hume and Adam Smith, the two Enlightenment philosophers who,
along with John Locke, had the greatest impact on economic thinking.

other thinker with a comparable influence on the architects of the United States' Constitution was Montesquieu. In his book *The Spirit of Law* from 1748, Montesquieu argues that the State's power ought to be divided. The laws should be formulated and amended by one branch of government (the legislative branch) and upheld by another (the judicial branch). The third branch (the executive branch) should take care of security and diplomacy.

In 1775, the time had come for Locke's and Rousseau's most radical thesis: People are entitled to rid themselves of rulers who do not sufficiently respect their interests. That idea, which Hobbes had resisted, was at the heart of the revolution of the United States during 1775–1783 as well as of the French revolution during 1789–1799.

Thinking about such institutional changes seems to require some notion of changing the game, which is the topic to which we turn next.

Food for Thought 7.1 *Anthropologists have long debated the transition from hunter-gatherer societies to agricultural societies. The evidence suggests that when farming became more popular, starting about 10,000 years ago, it was still being less productive in a purely technological sense. Rather, the advantage was that property rights were easier to establish, and to enforce once established. (i) Please explain this argument as plainly as possible. (ii) Suppose farming spreads gradually as new individuals change from being hunter-gatherers to being farmers. Each new farmer is thus better off with farming than with hunting. Must society as a whole be better off in the end?*

8
Changing the Game

What does it mean to change the game? Some examples are simple, at least on the surface. When a government changes the road speed limit or a soccer association modifies the off-side rule, the games have been changed for car drivers and soccer players. These examples are so easy to think about because the rule changes take place within a given regime of rule enforcement. Whatever traffic policing regime is in place, the enforcement of a 50 km/h speed limit is little different from the enforcement of a 60 km/h speed limit.

Just as standard decision theory explains the consequences of tax rate changes, game theory explains the consequences of different voting rules and trading mechanisms, such as different auction formats and priority schemes. In fact, under the assumption that the respective voting rules and market mechanisms are actually enforced, the theories are immensely powerful. Some of the greatest practical successes of microeconomic theory are in the field of market design.

But these are not the kind of rule changes that interest us here. We want to think more carefully about institutional phenomena such as the Meiji Restoration and the Scientific Revolution (see Chapter 5). How do dysfunctional institutions become replaced by better institutions? How do efficient and fair governments get to be established in the first place? In other words, how do societies escape from ".the state of nature" and acquire the sophisticated institutions that are required to sustain voting rules and trading rules, rather than succumbing to election manipulations and coups in the political sphere and to robbery or privilege and extortion in the economic sphere? To answer these questions, we cannot leave rule enforcement aside. To the contrary, enforcement might be the most important feature that institutional improvement needs to address.

Here we encounter a problem. How do we use game theory to study basic game changes? Game theory normally starts with a complete description of the game and presumes that the players know this description. The theory therefore does not admit the possibility that the players can change the game.[1] In terms of Figure 5.1, conventional game theory takes understandings and values for granted and therefore ignores institutional entrepreneurship.

Instead, what standard game theory does allow is to explain how the game *could be different*. For example, we can discuss understandings and values that might potentially improve behavior. Even if we lack a theory of institutional change, this will allow us to compare societies whose natural preconditions are similar but whose cultures – understandings and values – are different. That is, standard theory helps us to articulate what a social entrepreneur may seek to accomplish, but not how it is actually accomplished. Below, I will nonetheless talk about changing the game as if this were a well-defined concept.

---

[1] There are models that drop the "common knowledge" assumption, including an exciting literature on games with unawareness, but it's fair to say that these models have not yet made much of an impact on institutional analysis.

Expanding the Situation

We have already discussed how different values can account for different levels of prosperity. A society composed of rational selfish materialists will necessarily fail to reach the most desirable outcome in a social dilemma, in contrast with a society of sufficiently altruistic or dutiful people. What we shall now do is to begin to consider how different *understandings,* either alone or coupled with various values, can also affect material outcomes.

Most situations can realistically be expanded in at least three (complementary) ways.

- People can communicate.
- People can make transfers.
- People can hurt each other.

In particular, people can often communicate before they take their more impactful actions, and they can make monetary transfers both before and afterwards. Hurting others is usually only done afterwards, as punishment, although there are exceptions, such as imperialistic wars.

When I say that the situation has expanded, what I mean is simply that people think of the situation as including the possibilities for communication, transfers, and violence. When the situation is not expanded, people might still be aware of these possibilities, but they don't consider them to be a relevant part of the same situation.

For concreteness, suppose Rowena can make a sacrifice (play *S*) to help Colin. As Rowena decides whether to abide by the recommendation to help, she knows her decision might in principle affect Colin's willingness to make a transfer to her or to hurt her. Why? Because Colin will remember what she did and consider it relevant for his own choice, according to the practice of *reciprocity*. Reciprocity is the practice of rewarding good actions and punishing bad actions. We say people have a *desire for reciprocity* when either (i) they are filled with altruism toward people who perform good actions and spite toward people who perform bad actions, or (ii) they feel a duty to reward good behavior and punish bad behavior.

Obviously, reciprocal desires are only relevant when people remember the past and consider it relevant for today's choice. Colin must remember, and Rowena must believe that Colin will remember. What is perhaps more surprising is that there can sometimes be reciprocal behavior *without* reciprocal desires.

Enough said, it is time to prove that the above statements are true.

Positive Reciprocity

Suppose Colin can reward Rowena for helping by giving her a material compensation κ. In this case, the possible actions that comprise the situation are illustrated in Figure 8.1.

| S | 0, 2 |
| N | 1, 0 |

Stage 1

| | R | NR |
| $\kappa, -\kappa$ | 0, 0 |

Stage 2

Figure 8.1   Reward situation

Here, R denotes reward and NR no-reward. Let $1 < \kappa < 2$; i.e., the potential reward is greater than Rowena's cost and smaller than Colin's benefit. I call this the Reward situation, but we could also call it the Trading situation or the Trust situation.[2]

As usual, we cannot tell directly from the situation what the parties will do. We need to know their preferences. For simplicity, suppose Rowena is a selfish materialist.

---

[2] Unfortunately, it is common to refer to these kinds of situations as "Trust games." That, of course, invites the misunderstanding that the numbers are utilities.

Suppose first Colin is also a selfish materialist. In that case, the utilities are the same as the material payoffs.[3] We see from Figure 8.1 that Colin will not reward Rowena for helping. Forecasting Colin's behavior, Rowena will not help. The only equilibrium outcome is (N, NR).

Gratitude

Suppose instead Colin is not entirely selfish. After being helped, he is grateful and wants to reward Rowena. Formally, rewarding Rowena for helping creates a utility γ for Colin; think of γ as a "warm glow" Colin feels when he expresses his gratitude. In that case, the game is as in Figure 8.2:

S	0, 2
N	1, 0

Stage 1

$R(N)$	$R(S)$	NR
$\kappa, -\kappa$	$\kappa, -\kappa + \gamma$	0,0

Stage 2

Figure 8.2   Reward game with gratitude

Let $R(S)$ denote "playing R after Rowena played S" and $R(N)$ denote "playing R after Rowena played N." Suppose Colin's gratitude is strong enough to outweigh the material cost of rewarding, i.e., $\gamma > \kappa$. We then see from Stage 2 of Figure 8.2 that if Rowena has played S, Colin will play R, while if she has played N, Colin plays NR. Foreseeing this, Rowena will indeed play S rather than N. Even if she is selfish, she prefers to help Colin, because she understands that her short-term sacrifice will be more than compensated. Formally, the unique subgame-perfect equilibrium outcome is now (S, R).

Dutiful Reward

Colin might reward Rowena even if he does not feel true gratitude. Colin might have been told by his parents or teachers it is his duty to compensate others' sacrifice, and he feels guilty

---

[3] Recall that we have assumed players are risk neutral.

if he fails to do so. As before, let the parameter λ denote Colin's loyalty (dutifulness), and let μ denote the importance society ascribes to behaving justly. The game thus becomes as in Figure 8.3.

S	0,2
N	1,0

Stage 1

R	$NR(N)$	$NR(S)$
$\kappa, -\kappa$	0,0	$0, -\lambda\mu$

Stage 2

Figure 8.3 Reward game with positive reciprocity norm

Importantly, Colin's payoff to playing NR now depends on what Rowena did before. Let $NR(N)$ denote "playing NR after Rowena played N" and $NR(S)$ "playing NR after Rowena played S." If $\lambda\mu > \kappa$, Colin plays R if Rowena plays S, while he plays NR if Rowena played N. Thus, Rowena will indeed play S. Thus, the unique subgame-perfect equilibrium outcome is (S, R).

In other words, extending the game to allow transfers solves the problem if the person who needs help is known to be dutiful.

In this example, both gratitude and dutiful reciprocity ultimately benefit Colin, illustrating the broader lesson that morality can harmonize with material self-interest. In particular, it can be beneficial to be moral if others know about it. If Colin is known to be moral, Rowena trusts him; if he is known to be selfish, she doesn't trust him.

Negative Reciprocity and Punishment

An alternative to compensating Rowena for her sacrifice is punishing her in case she does not sacrifice. If punishment is possible, the situation becomes as in Figure 8.4.

S	0,2			P	NP
N	1,0			$-\pi,-\rho$	0,0
Stage 1				**Stage 2**	

Figure 8.4 Punishment situation

Here, P denotes punishment and NP no-punishment. Let $\pi > 1$ and $\rho < 2$. That is, Rowena's loss from being punished is greater than her cost of sacrificing, and Colin's cost of punishing is smaller than the benefit he obtains from Rowena's sacrifice.

If Colin is selfish, the Punishment game is the same as the Punishment situation; material payoffs and again utilities coincide. Let us apply backward induction to find out how the players will behave. At Stage 2, selfish Colin will not be willing to punish. Since he can avoid the punishment cost, he will play NP. If Rowena knows Colin is selfish, she will therefore play N. That is, the unique subgame-perfect equilibrium outcome of the Punishment game with selfish players is (N, NP).

Grievance

Many people get angry when they feel they are unjustly treated. Suppose Colin feels he is entitled to Rowena playing S. That is, he considers Play of N is forbidden. (If you want to make it feel more realistic that Colin is entitled to Rowena playing S, deduct 1 unit of payoff from Colin in each state, so that Rowena chooses between S yielding $(0, 1)$ and N yielding $(1, -1)$.)

In this case, Colin may feel an urge to punish Rowena in case she plays N. Formally, punishing Rowena after she has played N creates a utility γ for Colin (think of γ as a "warm glow" Colin feels when he expresses his grievance). In that case, the game is as in Figure 8.5:

$$S \quad \boxed{0,2} \qquad\qquad\qquad \begin{array}{ccc} P(N) & P(S) & NP \end{array}$$

	$P(N)$	$P(S)$	NP
	$-\pi, -\rho + \gamma$	$-\pi, -\rho$	$0,0$

$S \quad \boxed{0,2}$
$N \quad \boxed{1,0}$

Stage 1   **Stage 2**

Figure 8.5   Punishment game with grievance

Suppose Colin's utility from expressing his grievance is large enough to outweigh the material cost of punishing, i.e., $\gamma > \rho$. Then, if Rowena has played N, Colin will play P. If she has played S, Colin will play NP. Foreseeing this, Rowena will play S rather than N. Even if she is selfish, she prefers to help Colin, because she understands she will be punished otherwise. Formally, the unique subgame-perfect equilibrium outcome is now (S, NP).

Grievance can be a powerful feeling, and people sometimes make large sacrifices to get their revenge. Still, the role of grievance is often underestimated. For example, in the Vietnam War, the United States used intensive bombing to discourage the enemy. The strategy backfired, as more people became engaged in the resistance as a result.[4]

There also seems to be a cultural component to grievance. Here is a famous example. For a long time, homicide rates have been higher in the Southern US than in the North. Social psychologists proposed that this might be linked to a culture of honor that immigrants from lawless parts of Scotland and Ireland brought with them, and which made them prone to be easily enraged. Grosjean (2014) looked more closely at the data. She found that these immigrant groups indeed were more often involved in homicide, and that typical events were related to the defense of one's honor – but that the honor culture only survived in the US South. Why? Because the honor culture only persisted in areas where legal enforcement was weak. This is an environment where people have an advantage if they can credibly threaten to engage in punishment.

---

[4] Dell and Querubin (2018) cleverly prove this point by exploiting randomness caused by discontinuities in the US bombing strategy.

Note that grievance could matter even in situations that do not involve punishment. For example, suppose Colin normally cares for Rowena and would want to help her. One day, Rowena disappoints him. Then, Colin's grievance could lead him to withhold help.

Food for Thought 8.1 *One explanation for the support of Donald Trump as US President as well as for Brexit is that people who were harmed by globalization – especially the areas whose businesses lost out to Chinese competitors – blamed the economic and political elites. How might we conceptualize their grievance in terms of a utility function like (3.1)?*

Dutiful Punishment

It is also possible that society encourages Colin to punish Rowena if she does not help. This might seem extreme, but it is not unheard of. For example, on the French island Corsica people used to be shamed by family and friends if they did not avenge injustices.[5]

The relevant utilities are depicted in Figure 8.6.

S	0,2
N	1,0

Stage 1

P	$NP(S)$	$NP(N)$
$-\pi, -\rho$	0,0	$0, -\lambda\mu$

Stage 2

Figure 8.6 Punishment game with sanctioning norm

If $\lambda\mu > \rho$, Colin plays P if Rowena plays N and NP if she plays S. Thus, Rowena will play S. Again, extending the game to allow punishment solves the problem if the person who needs help is known to be dutiful.

---

[5] See Elster (1989, pp. 118–121) for this and other examples of societies that have had strong retribution norms.

Promise of Payment

Often, society fails to provide a social norm that stipulates a duty of helping. In these cases, people can create their own duties and norms of reciprocity through promises and threats. It costs nothing to make a promise, but suppose Colin suffers a utility loss of at least φ if he does not keep his promise (φ is the cost of making a false statement).[6]

Suppose Colin promises he will reward Rowena by paying κ, where $1 < \kappa < \varphi$. Call this action W, for giving the Word (of honor), and let NW denote not giving the Word. Figure 8.7 depicts the relevant actions.

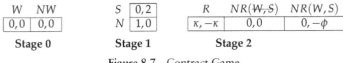

Stage 0   **Stage 1**   **Stage 2**

Figure 8.7   Contract Game

Note that Colin's payoff when he does not reward (plays NR) depends on whether he violates a promise or not (the strike-through (W, S), indicates all other strategies than (W, S)). As you may easily check (draw the game tree if you are unsure), the unique subgame-perfect equilibrium outcome is (W, S, R).

By contrast, if $\varphi < \kappa$, the promise is not credible. In this case, we say there is a *hold-up problem:* It is possible for Colin to compensate Rowena, but he finds it more profitable to renege on his promise of holding her up.

In other words, credibility of contractual promises can be provided by the morality of the contracting parties – by handshakes and words of honor. A promise solves the hold-up problem whenever the promisor's moral cost of breaking the promise outweighs the material gains.

---

[6] Many cultures place great emphasis on honesty and promise-keeping. Here is an enjoyable exercise: perform a quick internet search for relevant quotes from the Old Testament and from Confucius.

Religion offers one way to instil morality. Pathbreaking development economist Arthur Lewis (1955, p. 105) argues that religion can influence societies in many ways, of which honesty is one:

> If a religion lays stress upon material values, upon thrift and productive investment, upon honesty in commercial relations, upon experimentation and riskbearing ... it will be helpful to growth, whereas in so far as it is hostile to these things, it tends to inhibit growth.

It is hardly a coincidence that Quakers, who are known for the strength of their personal morality, were highly success-ful bankers.[7] Trust is essential in banking, and Quakers were more trustworthy than most.

Threat of Punishment

Promises of payment are friendly. They encourage coopera-tion through compensation. But Colin may also attempt to get Rowena's help without needing to compensate her. He could threaten instead.

Again, imagine Rowena is unaware she is able to help Colin, but Colin is aware. Colin may threaten her: "If you do not help, then I will punish you." As before, this can be described as a three-stage game. At Stage 0 Colin decides whether to threaten (give word, W) or not. At Stage 1, Rowena decides whether to help (sacrifice, S) or not. At Stage 2, Colin decides whether to punish (P) or not. Punishment inflicts a cost π on Rowena and a cost ρ on Colin. Not following through on a threat costs Colin φ.

The resulting game, the Coercion Game, is depicted in Figure 8.8.

---

[7] For example, Barclay's bank originated in 1690 as a private Quaker partner-ship, and Quakers were also central in founding Lloyds bank.

W	NW
0,0	0,0

Stage 0

S	0,2
N	1,0

Stage 1

P	NP(~~W,N~~)	NP(W,N)
$-\pi,-\rho$	0,0	$0,-\varphi$

Stage 2

Figure 8.8   Coercion Game

Suppose $\pi > 1$, so Rowena prefers helping to being punished, and $\varphi > \rho$, so Colin prefers to punish rather than not keeping his word. In that case, Colin will indeed coerce Rowena. That is, the unique equilibrium outcome is (W, S, NP).[8] Colin gets Rowena's help for free. He does not need to incur the cost of punishing her.

Other Promises and Threats

People can make promises about other actions than future transfers. They can also threaten other actions than punishment. For example, a common bargaining tactic is to make ultimatums: "If I do not get a sufficiently large share of the surplus, then I will walk away from the deal." Again, this ploy only works if the other parties believe the statement is credible. But what if both parties manage to make a credible commitment?

For concreteness, consider the case of bargaining between a trade union and the management of a firm.[9] Schelling (1956, p. 286) makes the following observation:

> ...it has not been uncommon for union officials to stir up excitement and determination on the part of the membership during or prior to a wage negotiation. If the union is going to insist on \$2 and expects the management to counter with \$1.60, an effort is made to persuade the membership not only that the management could pay \$2 but

---

[8] As usual, you might want to draw the game tree.

[9] The following paragraphs are taken almost word-for-word from Ellingsen and Miettinen (2014).

even perhaps that the negotiators themselves are incompetent if they fail to obtain close to $2. The purpose – or, rather, a plausible purpose suggested by our analysis – is to make clear to the management that the negotiators could not accept less than $2 *even if they wished to* because they no longer control the members or because they would lose their own positions if they tried.

That is, if the trade union's leader makes an explicit public proposal, and then immediately backs down from it, the leadership position is jeopardized. Hence, the public statement commits the leader, at least for some time.

As an empirical illustration, consider the 2004–2005 National Hockey League lockout. The lockout lasted 310 days and entailed the cancellation of 1,230 league matches that season. Revenue losses were approximately two billion US dollars, out of which about half would have been players' wages. The conflict started when NHL, led by Commissioner Gary Bettman, attempted to convince players to accept a new salary structure. The players' association, NHLPA, under executive director Bob Goodenow, considered the proposal to involve a salary cap, which the association had vowed never to accept. Eventually, however, as negotiations for the 2005–2006 season started, the union caved in and signed a new agreement. Bob Goodenow whose hardline stance against a salary cap contributed to the costly impasse, resigned from his position five days after the agreement was ratified.

Of course, Schelling's argument is not limited to labor negotiations. For example, strategic public statements often play a central role in territorial conflicts, as state leaders are usually reluctant to give up a publicly announced territorial claim. Such statements have severely limited the scope for subsequent negotiations over contested territories between Israel and Palestine, between India and Pakistan, as well as between several other nation-pairs.

To check you have properly understood both promises and threats, this is a good time to think about an observation by

Thomas Schelling (1960): "A promise is costly when it succeeds. A threat is costly when it fails."

Promises and threats are regularly in use: For example, when people organize their marriages, firms, and countries. But exactly why are promises being kept and threats upheld? So far, I have only offered one reason: People feel bad when they do not keep their word. That reason is obviously important. But there are other reasons too as we shall soon see.

Changing Understandings Only

Can people change the game to facilitate helping *without changing preferences*? In the examples above, the answer was negative. Promises of transfers and threats of punishments worked only because the promise or threat was associated with a desire to keep one's word.

But a promise does not need to involve a simple transfer. For example, suppose I want my partner to do something for me. The best thing I can promise in return might be to do a greater fraction of household chores. Household chores are tasks that need to get done by somebody; if my partner won't do them, then I will, and vice versa.

To lay out the logic of the argument as simply as possible, suppose Rowena and Colin find themselves in the following two-stage game:

Figure 8.9   Promise game

Note that the game at Stage 2 is the Distribution game of Figure 6.2. Suppose Rowena and Colin were originally planning to play Stage 2 without paying attention to Stage 1, and that they were going to play the equilibrium (*T*, *R*) which

Colin prefers. But now, before Rowena plays Stage 1, Colin makes the following proposal: "Dear Rowena! I know you don't want to make any sacrifice for me. But if you play S now, I promise I will play L afterwards. Of course, if you do not play S, we will just stick with the original plan, where I play R."

What will Rowena do? Suppose she believes Colin's promise. Then, by playing S followed by B, she gets utility $0 + 3 = 3$. By playing N followed by T, she gets utility $1 + 1 = 2$. Thus, if she believes the promise, she will do what Colin wants. Is the promise believable? Yes, if Colin believes that Rowena believes the promise, then he clearly wants to honor it: If he plays R instead of L after Rowena has played S, Colin gets 0 instead of 1.

Does Colin want to make the promise? Yes. If he makes the promise, he gets utility $3 + 1 = 4$. If he does not make it, he gets utility $0 + 3 = 3$.

Thus, the example shows how it is possible to improve the games people are playing. Two conditions are necessary, and I shall argue that both are amply fulfilled in practice.

First, players must be capable of changing what they will be actively remembering in the future. Surely, they are! Modern societies spend huge resources on creating accurate memories and on deciding what to do with them. People write contracts to recall what they have agreed. Firms' accounting consists of large systems for recording what has happened to cash flows (financial accounting) and who has contributed what (management accounting). Banks and insurance companies, as well as tax authorities, similarly rely on vast repositories of records of who has accomplished what.[10]

Second, the games people play in the future must have more than one equilibrium. I think this is the most realistic assumption of all. In Chapter 11, I explain why: Relationships are

---

[10] Laws on data protection, on the other hand, force us to forget some of this information. Reduced opportunities for cooperation represent a downside of these laws.

everywhere, and they are essentially mixed-motive games.[11] But for now, please trust me when I say there is nothing fishy about the Promise game in Figure 8.9.

Growing out of anarchy requires changing the game. But that is not all. It also requires playing a suitable equilibrium of the new game. After all, even the Promise game admits the equilibrium that the players act exactly as before. That is (T, R) is an equilibrium at Stage 2, and if Rowena expects (T, R) at Stage 2, then she will play N at Stage 1.

In the next chapter, we therefore address the question: How is coordination attained? Once we have an answer to that question, we can return to the debate between Hobbes on one side and Locke and Rousseau on the other on the best way to avert anarchy.

Food for Thought 8.2 *Nitin Nohria, Dean of Harvard Business School from 2010 to 2020, was a major proponent of the MBA Oath, a voluntary pledge that includes among other things a promise to "not advance my personal interests at the expense of my enterprise or society." What kind of problem does the MBA Oath seek to address? Do you think it can be successful?*

---

[11] It might also be argued that the best way to think about bargaining is that it is a game with many equilibria: See, e.g., Ellingsen and Robles (2002) and Ellingsen and Johannesson (2004a).

9

Coordination

We coordinate all the time. Meetings are held in a particular place and at a particular hour. People avoid crashing into each other on the street. Students working on a joint project decide who will do what. Parents ensure one of them will pick up from the daycare center. Manufacturers of complementary components ensure the components fit together.

Sometimes, coordination evolves spontaneously. People who like to chat over coffee may gradually coalesce to have coffee at the same time. At other times, coordination is an outcome of a long and rigorous process. Establishment of international technical standards can happen organically, but more often takes years of negotiation within and between standard-setting organizations.[1] And sometimes coordination happens fast, as when an officer gives orders, a manager provides directives, or a judge makes a decision.

---

[1] Please read https://en.wikipedia.org/wiki/Standards_organization. The article provides historical perspective, a wealth of examples, as well as an overview of standard-setting bodies. Similar organizations exist outside of manufacturing too. For example, the International Accounting Standards Board plays an important role for maintaining compatibility of firms' reporting.

We distinguish two classes of coordination problems. One class has common interests. That is, all players prefer the same equilibrium; we saw one example in Figure 6.1. Successful coordination on the best equilibrium is an instance of cooperation, as we defined it in Chapter 6. The other class has conflicting interests; we saw one example in Figure 6.2.

Common Interests

The most standard coordination game with common interests is depicted in Figure 9.1.

	H	L
H	2,2	0,0
L	0,0	1,1

Figure 9.1 Standard coordination game

Here, both players would always like to do the same as the other player, and they would rather both play H than L. For example, two friends would like to meet over a drink. Thus, they would like to go to the same bar. They prefer bar H to bar L, but they'd rather drink together in bar L than alone in bar H. In this case, it seems relatively easy to coordinate. Even if they have a history of going to bar L, they might simply talk to each other and agree to go to bar H. (You probably think this is obvious. In case you do not, hold on for one more example before you protest.)

Here is another common interest game.

	H	L
H	9,9	0,8
L	8,0	7,7

Figure 9.2 Stag Hunt game

In this game too, each player wants to do the same as the other. (If Colin plays L, Rowena wants to play L, and so on.) They also both prefer (H, H) to (L, L). Both these outcomes are Nash equilibria. However, unlike the game in Figure 9.1, the consequences of coordination failure are much worse for the player who has played H than for the player who has played L. The game is referred to as Stag Hunt, because of the discipline necessary for a group of hunters to catch a deer; both hunters must play the high action to succeed. If one of the hunters gets tempted to take a shot at a hare (the low action), the deer will be scared off and lost.[2]

Stag-hunt games reflect situations in which the weakest link has a large effect on the performance. There are many such situations. Meetings cannot start properly before all participants have arrived. A flight cannot depart until all the crew members are there. A soccer team plays much better if all ten outfield players perform their defensive duties diligently. In each case, everyone is perfectly willing to do their part, but only if they think it is very likely the others will do theirs.[3]

---

[2] The storyline is often attributed to Rousseau, but that's misleading. Rousseau was writing about how primitive people, who supposedly engaged in little planning, were able to hunt deer together. Rousseau's view was that their foresight was so limited that each hunter would be easily distracted by the presence of a hare:

> In this manner, men may have insensibly acquired some gross ideas of mutual undertakings, and of the advantages of fulfilling them: that is, just so far as their present and apparent interest was concerned: for they were perfect strangers to foresight, and were so far from troubling themselves about the distant future, that they hardly thought of the morrow. If a deer was to be taken, every one saw that, in order to succeed, he must abide faithfully by his post: but if a hare happened to come within the reach of any one of them, it is not to be doubted that he pursued it without scruple, and, having seized his prey, cared very little, if by so doing he caused his companions to miss theirs.
>
> (*Discourse on Inequality*, Part 2, Para. 9)

A proper representation of Rousseau's argument would thus require a dynamic game in which players heavily discount future payoffs. That game should have a unique equilibrium rather than posing a coordination problem. (We discuss some dynamic games in Chapter 11 and onwards, but not this one.)

[3] There are interesting extensions of this game to cases with more than two players. Then, it may be enough that a certain fraction of the players takes the

Let us assume all communication is cheap talk, in the sense that players are not bound to do what they say they will do. They have no qualms in breaking a promise. Should we then expect communication to help the hunters coordinate on the desirable outcome? To analyze this question, think of the game as a two-stage game, where Rowena can send a costless message at the first stage. The message either says "I intend to play H" or "I intend to play L."

One line of argument says yes. If Rowena pledges "I intend to play H" then Rowena has an additional reason to play H: If Colin believes the message, Colin will play H, and hence Rowena should play H too. We say the pledge to play H *is self-committing*.[4]

But, in the stag-hunt game, there is also a powerful counter-argument. Suppose Rowena thinks it is most likely that Colin will play L no matter what she says, but that Colin is somewhat more likely to play H if she says she intends to play H (for example, she thinks this message raises the probability Colin plays H from 0.2 to 0.4). What should Rowena say and do then? The answer is plain: Rowena should say she intends to play H because she is always better off if Colin plays H, but she should play L because that yields a higher expected utility. We say the pledge to play H *is not self-signaling*.[5] For a message to be truly credible it needs to be self-signaling.

By contrast, if you go back to the standard common-interest coordination game in Figure 9.1, you can check that Rowena's message that she intends to play H is both self-committing and self-signaling. There, it would just be stupid

---

"high" action. For example, even without government support, most banks can survive a mild bank-run where two percent of the customers simultaneously withdraw all their money. They would not survive if half the customers simultaneously sought to withdraw.

[4] A message is self-committing when the sender wants to do what she has said whenever (she believes) the receiver believes the message.

[5] The message is self-signaling if it is only sent when the sender intends to do what the message says.

of Rowena to say she intends to play *H* if she actually plans to play *L*.

Conflicting Interests

When games have conflicting interests, the need for a boss is stronger. Recall the Distribution game of Figure 6.2, repeated here for ease of reference:

	L	R
T	0,0	1,3
B	3,1	0,0

Figure 9.3   The Distribution game

Rowena prefers the equilibrium (*B*, *L*) and Colin prefers the equilibrium (*T*, *R*). Thus, if only Rowena gets to communicate before they play, she will say something like "I intend to play *B*." If only Colin gets to communicate, he will say "I intend to play *R*." But if both get to communicate on equal terms, and this is the conversation they have, they are no better coordinated than they would be without the communication.[6]

Making either Colin or Rowena the boss would remove the risk of coordination failure. Alternatively, they could engage a third person to be their superior and provide a recommendation or even a rule. When more than two persons are involved, there are several additional ways to select between equilibria. There could be a direct vote, or there could be a political assembly that has the right to decide.

---

[6] Careful analysis actually shows that such two-way pre-play communication can help players coordinate, but only a little. The reason is that symmetric equilibria involve mixed strategies; it is not an equilibrium to play (*B*, *R*) and it is not an equilibrium of the message stage for these messages to be sent with probability 1 either. As a result, the symmetric mixed strategy equilibrium of the game with pre-play communication yields somewhat higher expected utility than the corresponding equilibrium without communication.

A concrete example of such a coordination scheme was Sweden's decision to change from driving on the left (L) to driving on the right (R). Continued L-driving was considered problematic both because neighboring countries practiced R-driving and because most cars on Swedish roads were manufactured for the purpose of R-driving.[7] A referendum in 1955 yielded a large majority for retaining L-driving. However, in 1963, the Parliament nonetheless decided to change to R-driving, starting four years later.

Of course, compliance was not a problem. Everyone wants to drive on the same side of the road as others are driving. This is the ultimate example of a game with common interest. However, the implementation of the change from left to right required massive coordination and a lot of work. Each local municipality had to repaint road markings, move bus stops and traffic lights, redesign intersections, and to do it in such a way that traffic would flow smoothly both during the last week of L-traffic and during the first week of R-traffic.

During the night of Sunday September 3, 1967, most traffic was forbidden. Essential traffic first stopped at 04:50, then moved over to the other side of the road, before being allowed to drive on at 05:00. The transition worked perfectly.[8]

When people have conflicting interests, they do not always appreciate better coordination. Consider the game of Chicken (sometimes also called Hawk–Dove), which is displayed in Figure 9.4. We label the aggressive strategy H for Hawk and the unaggressive strategy D for Dove.[9] The Chicken game

---

[7] For a good description, see https://en.wikipedia.org/wiki/Dagen_H.

[8] Over the next few weeks, accidents went down quite significantly. However, after a few months, they had returned to their pre-reform level. One hypothesis was that frontal collisions on narrow roads would be permanently reduced when drivers in opposite directions came closer to each other, but it was not confirmed.

[9] The name Chicken originates from one of the applications of the game, where the two players are drivers who drive directly against each other. Unless one swerves, they both die. The one who swerves is a chicken (coward). Classic film renditions of Chicken are from *Rebel without a Cause* (1955) and *Mad Max I* (1979).

is similar to the Distribution game, in the sense that players have different preferences over the two pure-strategy equilibria. However, the non-equilibrium outcomes (H, H) and (D, D) are now different, with both players preferring the dovish outcome to the hawkish one.

$$
\begin{array}{cc|c|c|}
 & & D & H \\
\hline
D & & 3,3 & 1,4 \\
\hline
H & & 4,1 & 0,0 \\
\hline
\end{array}
$$

Figure 9.4   The Chicken (Hawk–Dove) game

In the present Chicken game, a coordinated outcome is clearly better than an uncoordinated outcome for the player who gets the high payoff of 4. However, the player who gets the low payoff of 1 might be better off without coordination. To see this, note that the mixed-strategy equilibrium of this game is for the players to (believe the opponent will) be playing each strategy with probability 1/2, as you may check by applying the same logic as in Footnote 8 of Chapter 6. This uncoordinated outcome yields an expected utility of 2. Experiments show people indeed take much less notice of each other's communication in Chicken than in Distribution.[10]

Chicken is an important game to consider because it potentially sheds light on wasteful conflicts, such as wars and strikes. The core idea is that a rational player may prefer to run the risk of a costly conflict rather than to accept a peace on poor terms.

Avoiding the mixed-strategy equilibrium of Chicken, just like avoiding the equilibrium outcome of the Prisoners' Dilemma, requires changing the rules of the game in a more fundamental way from merely allowing the players to talk to each other. In the Prisoners' Dilemma, talking doesn't help because there is no other equilibrium to coordinate on. In Chicken, talking doesn't help because nobody wants to listen.

---

[10] See He, S., Offerman, T. and Van de Ven, J. (2019): The power and limits of sequential communication in coordination games, *Journal of Economic Theory* 181, 238–273.

One way to extend the game would be to let a trusted third party do all of the communication in such a way that both Rowena and Colin would want to listen to the third party's message. Such mediation is often used to prevent strikes and wars.[11]

Common Awareness

In the discussion above, I was assuming all players are aware of the game. Actually, I assumed quite a bit more than that – I assumed the players have *common awareness* about the game. While that assumption is often a useful simplification, it sometimes blinds us to all the many phenomena that arise precisely in order to affect our common awareness. Much of what governments and company bosses do is to create common awareness, or to prevent it.

Again, a simple example highlights the difference between two persons both being aware of something and for them to have a common awareness.[12] Suppose Colin and Rowena are riding on a full bus on their way to a bar. Colin is standing near the front door and Rowena is standing near the rear door. Suddenly Rowena sees a mutual friend on the pavement

---

[11] Suppose Colin and Rowena have a common friend Max. Max speaks to both of them separately. His message to each will be either "play *H*" or "play *D*." Since Max cares for both, he would never tell both "play *H*." It is also no equilibrium that he always would tell both of them "play *D*" and both complies. A player only plays *D* if they think the other might be playing *H*. In the best symmetric equilibrium, Max tells both to play *D* with probability 1/3. The remaining time, Max either instructs Rowena to play *H* and Colin to play *D* or vice versa, each with probability 1/3. (The advanced reader might want to check that neither Rowena nor Colin has any incentive to deviate.) In expectation, Rowena and Colin thus each earn the payoff $(1 + 3 + 4)/3 = 8/3$. This is an improvement over the payoff of 2 which emerges without coordination. In fact, it is even better than $(1 + 4)/2 = 5/2$ they would earn on average by flipping a coin to determine who gets to play D. Thus, a mediator who speaks privately with the antagonists can do better than one who calls a meeting with both parties!

[12] This example is adapted from Michael Chwe's book *Rational Ritual*.

by the bus stop. The friend waves and points toward the pub on the corner. Rowena understands the friend wants to take them for a drink. Meeting the friend at the pub would be a better option for both Rowena and Colin than continuing on the bus and going to the original bar. Specifically, suppose going to the original bar yields the payoffs (1, 1) and going to the pub with the friend yields (2, 2), just as in the Standard coordination game in Figure 9.1. If one of them gets off the bus and the other stays on it, they get (0, 0). Compared to the Standard coordination game, the difference is that the players lack common awareness of the strategy H.

When should Rowena get off the bus? At first, you might think she should get off if she thinks Colin has seen the friend too. However, even if she can see Colin has seen the friend, that is of little use if she thinks Colin believes she has not seen the friend. In that case, Colin will stay on the bus because he believes Rowena will stay, and hence Rowena should also stay.[13] What is needed is for both of them to get eye contact, nod in the direction of the friend, and having thus established common awareness, jump off the bus and go to the pub.

Going for a drink might be important enough, but there are many other applications of this idea. Consider the problem of organizing a political protest. Protest organizers need to reach many people with their message, but that is not enough. Even if a large fraction of the people who get the message would like to participate if many others turn up, they may not want to come if they think others won't. Successful organization requires that many know (that many know ... etc.) that there will be a protest.

Advertisers seem to understand the power of common awareness. Products that are particularly valuable when many others also use them get systematically advertised at popular

---

[13] The problem closely resembles logical induction puzzles, like the Muddy Children Puzzle and the King's Wise Men Puzzle; see https://en.wikipedia.org/wiki/Induction_puzzles.

shows, thus creating a common awareness.[14] For example, take a look at the advertisers at Superbowl, the annual championship game of the National Football League (NFL), which often has the greatest viewership of all American broadcast during the year.[15] Among frequent product categories over the last couple of years are films (which are more fun when they can be discussed with others) and websites (which are more attractive when many others use them).

When a boss wants to implement a new policy, she will often call a meeting. Even if the information could be conveyed equally clearly in writing, one benefit of a meeting is that all the participants can see that the other participants are getting the information. Therefore, the worry is smaller that someone hasn't received the message or failed to pay attention to it. We would expect that meetings are used more intensively compared to other forms of communication when people need to coordinate than when people are less dependent on each other.

Sometimes, powerful people want to prevent coordination. When an autocrat seeks to quell the opposition, it is common to interfere with opportunities for communication. While cracking down on media and other platforms for social interaction might increase the magnitude of opposition, it reduces the main risk facing the autocrat: the risk of coordinated opposition.

Clarity

A final problem of coordination is that players misunderstand each other. They may be aware of the same reality, but they lack a sophisticated way of communicating.[16] A stark

---

[14] This example, too, is taken from Chwe (2001).

[15] See https://en.wikipedia.org/wiki/List_of_Super_Bowl_commercials.

[16] The television series *Fawlty Towers* is largely based on the hilarious miscoordination that may arise when people communicate poorly, especially

example is two people who do not speak the same language. For example, in the Distribution game 6.2, the ability to communicate may be of little value if the sender lacks the ability to describe which action she intends to choose, in a way that is understandable to the receiver. I believe this issue is of huge importance but, ironically, it is one area where we lack a common understanding of how we may best develop the analysis.[17]

Caveats

In this chapter, I have assumed that the players are selfish and rational. Some of the problems we have discussed would be smaller if players were less selfish and more moral. Coordination in Stag Hunt games would be easier if players were honest, and Stag Hunt situations would become less like Stag Hunt games and more like Standard coordination games if players were altruistic.

If players were less rational, coordination could become either easier or more difficult, depending on the situation and on the nature of irrationality. For example, naively believing what others say will tend to facilitate coordination on a desirable equilibrium when players have enough common interests, whereas it invites dishonesty and departure from equilibrium in several other cases.[18]

Food for Thought 9.1 *After 1989, many countries initiated a transition away from autocratic rule toward democracy. However, in several cases there was a subsequent backlash, and democratically elected governments were removed or turned to autocratic methods themselves. Researchers have*

---

when those like Basil Fawlty (the main character, played by John Cleese) believe they have made themselves clear.

[17] For a recent contribution and relevant references, see Gibbons et al. (2021).

[18] See, e.g., Ellingsen and Östling (2010); Ellingsen, Östling, and Wengström (2018).

found that such a backlash is most likely to occur in countries with weak democratic traditions. Please think about why the establishment of new democratic traditions may be more difficult than the maintenance of older democratic traditions.

Food for Thought 9.2 *According to sociologist Edgar Schein "Leaders work on the culture of the organization, creating it or changing it. Managers work within the culture of the organization." (i) How may we draw such a distinction between management and leadership using the concepts in this book? (ii) Is good management and leadership economically important? Or to be more precise: How might we best measure empirically the economic value of good management and leadership? (Exercise: Go to Google Scholar and search Bennedsen and Wolfenzon.)*

10

Authority's Limitations

Up until now, we have used the concept of a "boss" in the loose sense of who gets to speak or decide. Let me now be a little bit more careful, and define authority as follows:

Definition 5 *A player has nominal authority if the player's messages are supposed to be obeyed. A player has real authority if the player's messages are obeyed whenever they are consistent with equilibrium play.*

For example, in a monarchy, the monarch's word is the law. On a ship, the captain's orders cancel out orders from any other officer. Thus, the monarch has nominal authority over all subjects, and the captain has nominal authority over all the crew.

Nominal authority is neither necessary nor sufficient to guarantee real authority. Sometimes, people will listen more to informal leaders than to formal leaders. Indeed, we have words for describing instances where formal authority is challenged by competing informal authorities. Kings can lose their authority in an insurrection or a revolution, captains lose theirs in a mutiny.

The strength of a leader's authority relies on what each follower believes that other followers believe. In the time of strong monarchies, an important role of castles, statues, coronations, and other royal artefacts and events was to create a shared belief in the monarch's authority. To the extent that there may arise challengers, it is equally important to undermine belief in their authority.[1]

Throughout history, many monarchs have set themselves above the law. Laws are applied only to subordinates. In such sovereign monarchies, the king's word *is* law. A sovereign monarch's authority is then absolute in the following sense:

Definition 6 *A player has absolute authority in the entire game if at any stage the player can (use communication to) induce her preferred equilibrium – albeit only among the equilibria that are consistent with the exercise of absolute authority at remaining stages.*

That is, any constraint on the king's authority comes in the form of future statements, not in the form of past statements.

Hobbes argued that such sovereign power might be, if not good, then at least the lesser of the relevant evils. As we have seen, Locke, Rousseau, and Montesquieu disagreed. To shed some light on the debate, consider again the Promise game in Figure 8.9, repeated below:

S	0,3
N	1,0

Stage 1

	L	R
T	0,0	1,3
B	3,1	0,0

Stage 2

Figure 10.1   Promise game

---

[1] When King Charles II of England got back his Crown in 1660, after Oliver Cromwell's son Richard proved incapable of continuing his father's reign as a military dictator, Charles wanted to warn others not to undermine his rule. Oliver Cromwell's dead body was dug up from its grave and subjected to a posthumous execution. His body was hanged in chains and then thrown into a pit. His head was cut off and displayed on a pole outside Westminster Hall for about 25 years.

Please think hard about the following question:

Exercise 10.1 *(i) Suppose Colin has absolute authority. Which payoffs will Rowena and Colin obtain? (ii) Suppose Rowena has absolute authority. Which payoffs will Rowena and Colin obtain?*

As we have already shown in Chapter 8, there exists an equilibrium in which Colin earns 4. When Colin has absolute authority, he only earns 3. Thus, Colin is better off if some of his authority is taken away from him!

The reason is simple. You can only make credible promises if something stops you from breaking the promise in the future. And authority can be more likely to help you to break the promise than to keep it. Authority gives rise to a hold-up problem. As Niccolò Macchiavelli formulated it more than 500 years ago in *The Prince* (Ch. 18): "A Prince never lacks legitimate reasons to break his promise." It can be better for everyone if the authority of contracts trumps the authority of individuals.

It has been claimed that this kind of mechanism contributes to explaining the economic development of England after the Glorious Revolution of 1688. At that point, the Crown was forced to cede power to the Parliament. Also, the courts became more independent of the Crown, and the Bank of England was established to keep proper track of the Crown's debts. Previously, rich people avoided lending to the untrustworthy Crown. Now, they became eager to make such safe investments.[2] In comparing the philosophy of Hobbes, and his arguments in favor of a sovereign ruler, to Locke and Rousseau, and their arguments against such unfettered sovereign powers (as we discussed in Chapter 8), this evidence

---

[2] For a full account of this argument, see North and Weingast (1989). An alternative interpretation is that the Glorious Revolution was only one of many instances where the power of the Crown was kept in check, and not a particularly important one; see Ogilvie and Carus (2014).

favors the latter. Locke's analysis is particularly impressive. Writing in 1689, he did not have the privilege of observing the long-run fallout of the Glorious Revolution available to Rousseau.

Changing authority can be difficult, not least because legal rules will be interpreted by powerful people. In 2008, Russia's president Vladimir Putin had served two terms and was ineligible for a third term. However, one day after the election of Dmitry Medvedev to the post, Putin was appointed Prime Minister. In that role, he was able to command the *real* authority that would normally be associated with the presidency. Putin subsequently regained the presidency through rigged elections in 2012 and 2018, after the term limits had been increased in an amendment of the Constitution in 2008.

Food for Thought 10.1 *Should music conductors be authoritarian? Probably: Researchers have recorded violinists' and conductors' movement kinematics during execution of Mozart pieces. They show that an increase of conductor-to-musicians influence, together with the reduction of musician-to-musician coordination (an index of successful leadership) goes in parallel with quality of execution, as assessed by musical experts' judgments.*

11

Relationships

The Promise game in Figure 8.9 was designed to clarify why selfish and immoral people can make credible promises. But its structure is rather special. How often can people make promises with the help of future games with multiple equilibria? The answer might surprise you: whenever players interact without a definite end, anticipated future interactions between the same players are often best understood as a game with many equilibria.

To illustrate the power of long-term relationships, begin by studying the Reward situation again (I have changed the payoffs a little, but not the logic). Let players be selfish. Thus, it is also a Reward *game*.

S	0,3
NS	1,0

Stage 1

R	NR
2,0	0,2

Stage 2

Figure 11.1 Reward game (Trading game)

At Stage 1, Rowena either sacrifices (plays *S*) or not (plays *NS*), just as before. Note that her only reason to sacrifice is that she hopes to be rewarded in the future. Thus, I shall also refer to the choice of S as Rowena trusting Colin. At Stage 2, Colin either rewards Rowena's trust (plays R) or does not reward it (plays NR). Therefore, this game is commonly called a Trust game.

Alternatively, we may call it the Trading game.

Exercise 11.1 *(i) If the Reward game is played once, which subgame-perfect equilibria does it have? (ii) If it is played ten times, how many equilibria does it have?*

But suppose now that every time Rowena meets Colin, they know there may be a next time. Importantly, both of them think they will remember what has happened in the past when they meet in the future. At first blush, the resulting game may look incredibly difficult to study. As the past becomes longer, there are more past events to condition the current action on. Thus, the set of strategies grows exponentially. (Remember that Colin already has four strategies when they only interact once.) But, by asking the right kinds of questions, it turns out we can still say a lot about the players' opportunities to cooperate.

If you are new to game theory, the next two pages may feel like a tough challenge. If you just read carefully, you will still manage.

The Threat of Terminating the Relationship

The first point I want to convey is that relationships are powerful because they can be prematurely terminated. If you have something wonderful, you don't want to run the risk of losing it.

For simplicity, suppose there is a constant probability $\delta < 1$ that the game will repeat itself (if it has not already ended), and that there is no risk that the game breaks down between the two stages. If δ is large, the game itself is therefore unlikely to end. Suppose Rowena and Colin play the following pair of strategies in each period:

- (Rowena): play *S* if always (*S*, *R*) in the past; otherwise play *NS*;
- (Colin): play *R* if *S* this period and always (*S*, *R*) in the past; otherwise play *NR*.

These strategies are called "grim trigger" strategies, because it only takes one failure to behave cooperatively for cooperation to be withdrawn forever. At the same time, the strategies do grant the opponent the benefit of the doubt. No player plans to be the first not to cooperate. The interesting result is this: If δ is sufficiently large, this pair of strategies constitutes an equilibrium. That is, cooperation between rational players is possible when the horizon is indefinite, despite being impossible when the horizon is finite.

The proof has two important steps. The first step is to identify the deviations we need to consider. As it turns out, it is enough to check that no player has an incentive to make a single-period deviation.[1] Rowena clearly has no reason to deviate to *NS*, since that entails a loss of payoff already within the period (she gets 1 instead of 2). The second step is therefore merely to check that Colin does not have an incentive to play the deviation *NR* this period.

Let us make the computation Colin faces: He has already obtained 3 this period. By playing *R* Colin sacrifices 2, but obtains a net payoff of 3 − 2 = 1 in each future period the game continues. By playing *NR*, he does not make the sacrifice, but will get 0 in all future periods. Since the probability that the relationship lasts (at least) *t* future periods is δ^t, Colin will play *R* if

$$\delta + \delta^2 + \delta^3 \ldots \geq 2, \qquad (11.1)$$

---

[1] This follows from a fundamental result of dynamic programming, which I shall not try to explain here.

which is equivalent to[2]

$$\delta \geq 2/3.$$

In other words, Colin prefers to play R as long as the probability that the relationship continues is at least 2/3.

The logic is that the indefinite game that Rowena and Colin will play in the future has multiple equilibria. In particular, playing (NS, NR) forever is an equilibrium, just as playing (NS, NR) in the single-period game is. Therefore, the players can credibly threaten themselves that their relationship will permanently turn sour unless each of them behaves well.

Note that the grim trigger threat is not the only threat that will work. If δ is sufficiently large, Colin can be deterred from cheating even if the relationship turns sour only for a few periods. Such short-term punishments are preferable when players can fail to cooperate by mistake, or if there is a risk of misperceiving or misremembering the other player's action.

The analysis shows that entirely selfish people may cooperate even if there are short-run gains from pursuing one's own interest. If they only expect to interact frequently enough with each other, any game becomes a coordination game.[3] In particular, this insight helps us to make sense of cooperation between criminals and between countries. In both cases, the parties need to govern their own relations, as there is no police or other third party they can turn to.

What if people are not entirely selfish? For example, suppose Colin values Rowena's payoff at α per unit, where α is a

---

[2] In case you have never worked with infinite series before, note that the expression $\delta + \delta^2 + \ldots$ is easy to rewrite (this is a typical geometric series, so it's a useful trick to learn). Simply denote the expression's value x. Then, by factoring out δ, you see immediately that $\delta + \delta x = x$, which implies $x = \delta/(1-\delta)$. Now you can just rearrange to solve the inequality $x \geq 2$ for δ.

[3] Of course, this does not imply that feelings are irrelevant for cooperation. Altruism reduces the temptation to cheat, and anger (temporary spitefulness) reduces any temptation an altruist may feel to cut the punishment short.

constant between 0 and 1. That is, Colin is somewhat altruistic toward Rowena. In analogy with (11.1), Colin is now
willing to play R as long as

$$\delta(1 + \alpha) + \delta^2(1 + \alpha) + \delta^3 + \ldots \geq 2.$$

Using the same logic as in Footnote 2, we find the critical
value for δ has now declined from 2/3 to

$$\delta \geq \frac{2}{3 + \alpha}.$$

When people are kinder toward each other, they are less
tempted to cheat in a relationship.

Still, the possibility of cooperation is only that: a possibility. Just as in the simple coordination games we studied in
Chapter 9, cooperation requires mutual faith. The indefinitely
repeated Trading game retains the equilibrium outcome of the
one-shot game. That is, regardless of the patience δ, it is an
equilibrium that Rowena plays S and Colin plays NS every
period.[4] David Hume (1740, Book III, Part II, Section V) captures the problem magnificently:

> Your corn is ripe today; mine will be so tomorrow. 'Tis
> profitable for us both, that I shou'd labour with you to-day,
> and that you shou'd aid me to-morrow. I have no kindness
> for you, and know you have as little for me. I will not,
> therefore, take any pains upon your account; and shou'd I
> labour with you upon my own account, in expectation of a
> return, I know I shou'd be disappointed, and that I shou'd
> in vain depend upon your gratitude. Here then I leave you
> to labour alone: You treat me in the same manner. The
> seasons change; and both of us lose our harvests for want
> of mutual confidence and security.

---

[4] If you don't believe me, please check the logic for yourself. It is a nice exercise,
and rather simple too if you worked through the example above.

According to Hume, civilization depends on moving away from this inefficient equilibrium to the efficient equilibrium, in which the (still selfish) farmers have learned to have more trust in each other.[5]

"Well," you might say, "I see that Hume understood that the indefinitely repeated game has an equilibrium in which people fail to cooperate. But could he really have understood the logic underpinning the cooperative equilibrium? Is it possible that a 29-year-old, living in 1740, using plain words only, could deduce this result?" It is. Let me quote the end of the subsequent paragraph:

> Hence I learn to do a service to another, without bearing him any real kindness; because I foresee that he will return my service, in expectation of another of the same kind, and in order to maintain the same correspondence of good offices with me or with others. And accordingly, after I have serv'd him, and he is in the possession of the advantage arising from my action, he is induc'd to perform his part, as foreseeing the consequences of his refusal.

The Threat of Punishment

Now we understand how the threat of letting the relationship turn sour can work to support cooperation. The next step is to understand how threats of punishment can support cooperation. Consider the following game.

S	0,3
NS	1,0
Stage 1	

R	NR
2,0	0,2
Stage 2	

P	$-\rho, -\pi$
NP	0,0
Stage 3	

Figure 11.2   A Trust game with punishment

[5] Hume's example is slightly different from the Trading game as the farmers' roles are symmetric. Every second period Colin can sacrifice for Rowena, and in the remaining periods Rowena can sacrifice for Colin. A good exercise is to find the critical value of δ that allows cooperation in this case.

The first two stages are the same as before. The third stage is new. Here, Rowena can punish Colin (the labels P and NP denote punish and not punish respectively). The punishment is costly not only to Colin, but also to Rowena. The parameter ρ (rho) denotes Rowena's cost of punishing (i.e., retaliating, hence the name ρ) and the parameter π denotes Colin's cost of being punished.

Exercise 11.2 *(i) If the Trust game with punishment is played once, which subgame perfect equilibria does it have? (ii) If it is played ten times, how many equilibria does it have?*

Suppose now, as in the previous chapter, that there is a constant probability $\delta < 1$ that the game will repeat itself (if it has not already ended), and that there is no risk that the game breaks down between the three stages of a period. For simplicity, suppose there is no altruism between the players, i.e., $\alpha = 0$. Can we construct an equilibrium in which the punishment threat is useful? The answer is yes.

Clearly, the point of Rowena's punishment threat is to ensure that Colin rewards Rowena's trust. What is the best way to formulate such a threat? It might be tempting to think that Rowena should make the punishment threat as grim as possible: i.e., that she should threaten both to stop trusting and to punish indefinitely if Colin ever fails to reward her trust. However, while this punishment would be devastating to Colin, it is not credible, because Rowena has no reason to carry it out. If the relationship is ending, punishment is just a waste of Rowena's resources.

So, if punishment is to have any value for Rowena, it must be accompanied by a continuation of the relationship.[6] That is, we must think of the threat of costly punishment as an alternative to breaking off the relationship. Let us therefore consider the following strategy profile:

---

[6] Recall that we abstract from any consideration of anger and spite that Colin's misbehavior might have caused in Rowena.

- Stage 1 (Rowena): play S if always either (S, R) or (S, NR, P) in the past; otherwise NS;
- Stage 2 (Colin): play R if S this period and always either (S, R) or (S, NR, P); in the past; otherwise NR;
- Stage 3 (Rowena): play P if (S, NR) this period and always either (S, R) or (S, NR, P) in previous periods; otherwise play NP.

These strategies are similar to before, in the sense that both players behave nicely as long as they always have done so in the past. But now, they also play nicely if any deviation has been punished in the same period. The relationship only breaks down after a failure to apply immediate punishment.

Do these strategies form an equilibrium? As before, we need to consider whether there are any profitable one-step deviations. Stages 1 and 2 are trivial to check: Stage 1, as before Rowena is perfectly willing to trust Colin, since the cost this period is only 1 and the benefit is 2. At Stage 2, Colin weighs the benefit on a single period's transgression, which is 2, against the cost of being immediately punished, which is π. Thus, Colin willingly plays R if $\pi \geq 2$. The more interesting question concerns Stage 3. Is Rowena willing to punish if Colin has transgressed? Punishment costs Rowena p today, but failing to punish costs her $2 - 1 = 1$ every subsequent period (since the relationship is then supposed to break down). Therefore, she is willing to punish as long as

$$-p + 2\delta + 2\delta^2 + \ldots \geq \delta + \delta^3 + \ldots,$$

or equivalently[7]

$$p \leq \frac{\delta}{1 - \delta}. \tag{11.2}$$

That is, punishment must not be too costly relative to the

---

[7] To perform this computation, recall the trick in Footnote 2.

expected future gains. If the relationship is unlikely to last long (δ is small), Rowena is not willing to engage in very costly punishment to rescue it.

How low must ρ be in order for the punishment option to have value? Without punishment, we know cooperation was sustainable whenever $\delta \geq 2/3$. If we insert $\delta = 2/3$ into (11.2), we see that it becomes $\rho \leq 2$. That is, whenever ρ is smaller than 2, the threat of punishment can help sustain cooperation in some cases when the threat of breaking up the relationship is insufficient to do so.[8]

Food for Thought 11.1 *Many committees will have a secretary who takes notes ("minutes of the meeting"). Often, one or more members will be appointed to verify the accuracy of these minutes. At the next committee meeting, all the members will then have an opportunity to discuss whether the minutes are acceptable, after which the minutes are archived. Please use the above concepts to think about the purpose of such procedures, in particular whether they may be contributing to improve resource allocation and if so how.*

Food for Thought 11.2 *In 1996, the President of South Africa, Nelson Mandela, created the Truth and Reconciliation Commission. Its task was to investigate crimes committed under apartheid by both the government and the ANC. To prevent the creation of martyrs, the Commission granted individual amnesties in exchange for testimony of crimes. What were the possible benefits of such a commission?*

---

[8] But note that punishment should not be observed in these equilibria; threats are only costly when they fail. When would we observe punishment in equilibrium? As indicated in the previous chapter, players could make mistakes, or their actions might be observed with noise. It is also possible that parameters vary stochastically. For example, if Colin temporarily finds it very costly to play R, he will find it optimal to deviate today even if he is aware that the cost might be lower again tomorrow. (The latter scenario may be relevant for the relationship between a drug addict and a dealer, for example.)

12

Third-Party Punishment

We are now ready to discuss why players may want to purchase punishment rather than relying on their own ability to punish. That is, we can finally discuss such important social institutions as the Mafia and the State and how they enable markets.

Let us continue our analysis of the Trust game with a punishment option from the previous chapter. Suppose now that punishment is prohibitively costly for Rowena to engage in; her cost of retaliating is $\rho > 2$. Moreover, let δ (the probability that the relationship continues), be moderate or low: $\delta < 2/3$. Thus, Rowena has no threat that is potent enough to deter Colin from breaking his promise to reward her trust. Even if she breaks off the relationship in case Colin does not reward her trust, Colin is not deterred by that threat since the relationship is likely to break down soon anyway.

In other words, Rowena is unable to discipline Colin on her own. If we think of Rowena as a potential producer and seller and Colin as a customer, you see that this is a bad situation: Industry does not get off the ground for lack of institutional support; the market is unsustainable.

Professional punishers, henceforth called enforcers, can fill this void. There are two reasons why such enforcers may be willing to engage in punishment even though Rowena is not. The first is that they may have a better punishment technology, i.e., a lower cost ρ_E or a more painful effect π_E; we neglect this reason here. The second is that they may sell their service to many clients. There are two notable features of this argument.

The reason why it is possible for enforcers to have many clients is that punishment threats are not costly when they succeed; the successful enforcer never needs to do any work!

The second benefit associated with multiple clients is this: The enforcer is more eager to carry out punishment when more money is at stake. The enforcer that fails to punish is likely to lose not only the client who is being let down, but also other clients who suspect that they will not be protected either. Thus, a large stock of well-paying clients is the best guarantee that the enforcer will be diligent.

Together, these special features of the enforcement business imply that it is a so-called *natural monopoly*, where overall costs are lowest when there is a single supplier of protection services.

Let us now articulate these arguments more formally. To do so, I need to slightly alter the interpretation of the relationship and in particular the continuation probability δ. Let us now interpret $(1 - \delta)$ as the probability that any single player needs to quit the relationship. However, if one player quits, there will always come a new player to take that player's place, and this new player will have access to the whole history of the game. Thus, each player's reason for discounting future payoffs is that the player herself might need to leave the game, not that she is deserted by somebody else. For example, if a shop-owner has a health problem, somebody else will take over the shop, so the customer isn't left unable to trade. To keep notation simple, I assume all players have the same continuation probability δ.

I also extend the model in two ways. First, to allow enforcers to have multiple clients, I now assume there are

$n \geq 2$ Rowena–Colin pairs. Second, to allow enforcers to earn money, I add a Stage 0 where clients (Rowenas) decide whether to pay their enforcer or not. From now on, let me follow Dixit (2003) and refer to each enforcer as Enfo. Let f denote the fee Enfo asks for, let F denote paying the fee and let NF denote not paying. For a Rowena–Colin–Enfo interaction, each period can thus be visualized as follows:

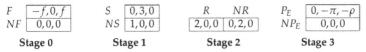

Figure 12.1   A Trust game with professional punishment

Here, I have added Enfo's utility as the third number in each cell. Note that now it is Enfo who is supposed to act at Stage 3. Hence, I denote punishment P_E and non-punishment NP_E.

Here are the equilibrium strategies I described informally above:

- Stage 0 (Rowena): play F if never NP_E after F and NR for any (potentially different) Rowena–Colin pair; otherwise NF;
- Stage 1 (Rowena): play S if F this period; otherwise NS;
- Stage 2 (Colin): play R if (F, S) this period; otherwise NR;
- Stage 3 (Enfo): play P_E if (F, S, NR) this period; otherwise NP.

If you understand Stage 0, you will understand the rest. At Stage 0, each Rowena decides whether to pay the fee f or not. The proposed strategy says that she pays whenever Enfo has never failed to deliver justified and paid-for punishment.[1] She stops paying fees if Enfo fails to punish adequately.[2]

---

[1] I could have introduced extra indices to differentiate between the Enforcer's clients, but the notation gets more cluttered.

[2] At this point, you might want to ask a critical question: How can one client know whether another client has paid her fee, and thus is worthy of protection? If you have watched Mafia films, you may have seen the answer.

Let us now investigate whether the strategy profile forms an equilibrium. As always, we only need to check whether any single player has an incentive to deviate in a single period given that other players stick to their proposed strategies.

At Stage 0, consider Rowena's decision to pay (play F) when that is the prescription. The choice is easy. If she does not pay (plays NF), her payoff is 1 this period and $2 - f$ in all future periods. If she does pay, she earns $2 - f$ this period as well. Therefore, Rowena's best decision is to play F as long as $f < 1$.

At Stage 1, Rowena's decision is trivial. If she hasn't paid the fee, Colin is not going to reward her trust, so it's better to play NS. If she has paid the fee, Colin will reward her trust, so she is better off playing S.

At Stage 2, Colin's decision resembles the case when Rowena did the punishing herself; following (F, S) by Rowena, he rewards trust (plays R) if the punishment is sufficiently harsh, i.e., if $\pi \geq 2$.

At Stage 3, Enfo is only asked to punish if Colin has deviated. Suppose he has. Then, if Enfo fails to punish, the earnings are 0 forever after. If Enfo punishes, all clients will continue to pay. Suppose Enfo has m clients. Then, the expected value of future payments are

$$mf(\delta + \delta^2 + ...) = mf \frac{\delta}{1 - \delta}.$$

Thus, Enfo is willing to punish whenever

$$\rho \leq mf \frac{\delta}{1 - \delta}. \tag{12.1}$$

Comparing (12.1) to (11.2), we see that Enfo has a greater incentive to punish than Rowena did if (and only if) $mf > 1$.

The Mafia is usually quite explicit about which businesses stand under their protection and which do not. Likewise, the business itself is eager to explain to potential robbers or delinquent customers that it stands under protection.

Since Rowena is willing to pay as long as $f \leq 1$, the market is thus easier to sustain with a professional enforcer as long as that enforcer has more than one client.

Exercise 12.1 *Consider a version of the Trust game in Fig. 12.1 with two potential enforcers, and parameters $\rho > 2$, $\delta < 2/3$. Each can earn 0 per period by not being an enforcer. Suppose that, before the rest of the game starts, each potential enforcer i offers to protect each Rowena in every period that the respective Rowena pays a fee f_i. What is the lowest fee that is offered and accepted in any Nash equilibrium in which the market is sustained through professional enforcement?*

You may be tempted to answer $f_i = 0$. After all, if one enforcer can get all the protection business at a positive fee, that enforcer earns a profit, whereas the potential competitor earns nothing. But the answer is wrong. The lowest fee that is compatible with trade when the enforcer has m clients is

$$f(m) = \frac{(1 - \delta)\rho}{\delta m}. \tag{12.2}$$

This equation simply solves Equation 12.1 for f. Observe that this fee is declining in m. Thus, the fee is as small as possible when m is as large as possible, namely $m = n$. Thus, the answer to Exercise 12.1 is

$$f^* = \frac{(1 - \delta)\rho}{\delta n}. \tag{12.3}$$

The idea is obvious once you think about it: The expected total value of future fees must be high enough for the enforcer to engage in punishment when called upon to do so. Therefore, the more clients a professional enforcer has, the lower is the fee that each client of that enforcer needs to pay in order to keep the enforcer motivated.

If the enforcement business is split up among multiple enforcers, each enforcer will have fewer than n clients, and hence will have to charge a fee above $f(n)$ to credibly promise to punish. Therefore, enforcement is a natural monopoly.

Since any enforcer who has clients earns a positive profit – and does not even need to do anything if everyone believes the threat – it is an attractive profession. There is also a strong temptation to get rid of potential rivals, in which case a monopoly enforcer might be able to charge even more than f^*. Since enforcement is a winner-takes-all profession, we should not be surprised the competition is often violent; real-life Enfo has often been a successful war lord.

The clients, on the other hand, would prefer to organize a peaceful competition between potential monopoly enforcers and insist on a fee of around f^*.[3] Political elections in democratic societies represent such a competition. Each potential ruler makes election promises, voters vote, and then every shop owner pays their fees (taxes) to the election winner. Voting becomes a coordination game, in which a natural equilibrium is for people to vote for a candidate that charges low taxes (albeit not lower than the level required to fulfill the enforcement promise). Even though promises and votes are instances of virtually costless communication, this coordination mechanism has the potential to replace bloody warfare with peaceful politics as a means for allocating power.

One generalization seems especially important. We have assumed all participants consider the continuation probability δ to be the same. However, an enforcer's horizon typically differs from the horizon of others. In particular, if Enfo is likely to be successfully challenged in the future, δ_E is smaller than δ_C and δ_R. Since it is δ_E that determines f^*, we see it could

---

[3] The enforcer here is more easily interpreted as a local authority figure, protecting subjects against each other, than as a king protecting subjects against foreigners. However, the model might also be useful for thinking about how a central enforcer could keep regions from fighting each other.

be in the interest of Colin and Rowena to increase δ_E. Literal cut-throat competition between enforcers benefits nobody, as a more insecure Enfo requires greater fees to make a credible promise of protection.

This logic might explain why people have accepted hereditary monarchy. A ruler who thinks that family members will take over the privilege will require a lower level of taxes in return for protecting the territory than a ruler whose power base is challenged – especially when the challenge comes not only from external threats (rulers of neighboring territories), but also from the people under protection. In Mancur Olson's (1993) memorable phrasing, a stationary bandit is preferable to a roving bandit.

While democratic elections tend to limit the expected duration of governments, they also potentially reduce the opportunity of the elected leaders to enrich themselves. In order to clarify the trade-off between increasing δ_E and the danger that Enfo attempts to raise f above $f^*(\delta_E)$, we would need to model both democracy and autocracy in greater detail. For example, if people are going to elect their ruler, we need to take account of the possibility that the ruler will be able to "bribe" parts of the electorate and fund the bribe by charging $f > f^*$.

Up until now, my depiction of third-party enforcers has been brutal, but benign. I argued that enforcers arise because people are not interacting sufficiently frequently to resist the temptation to cheat each other. This picture is too rosy. Potential enforcers also have an incentive to nurture distrust, that is to reduce altruism a as well as to prevent people from organizing around a cooperative equilibrium – for example by destroying opportunities for communication.[4] That is,

---

[4] As documented by Pagden (1988) and Gambetta (1988a) among others, both kings and mafias have been using such divide-and-conquer strategies to keep up the demand for their services. Here is a quote from Gambetta (1988b, p. 173):

> The mafioso himself has an interest in regulated injections of distrust into the market to increase the demand for the product he sells – that is,

low-trust societies can be the deliberate creation of rulers who would otherwise not be able to charge a substantial price for their governance.

Collective Responsibility

The theory tells us that the frequency of interaction is crucial. It is easier to sustain cooperation between parties who meet each other often, for example between family members or neighbors. But often the gains from trading are greatest with people who live far away. Distant communities have access to resources that we lack, and vice versa. In this case, each community may be able to enforce law and order internally, but how have people been able to trade across distant communities?

For much of our history, the answer is collective responsibility. Greif (2006b) gives a clear example: In 1323 the goods of a merchant from London, John de Grantham, were transported through the important English port of Dover. The goods are confiscated. While de Grantham has done nothing wrong, he comes from London. As it turns out the Mayor of London has failed to collect a debt that a Londoner, Henry Nasard, had failed to pay to William Virgil of Dover. In other words, if the London Mayor wants to protect the goods of his trader John de Grantham, he better make sure that Henry Nasard's debt is paid first. By treating all Londoners as part of a collective, the community of Dover can exercise control over the citizen of London, Henry Nasard who wronged the citizen of Dover, William Virgil.

Note the analogy to clan rule. The point of a clan is precisely to carry a collective reputation. If one is hurt, all are hurt. If one does something wrong, all have done something

protection. If agents could trust each other independently of his intervention he would, on this score at least, be idle. The income he receives and the power he enjoys are the benefits to him of distrust.

wrong. In the absence of an enforcer that can maintain order by disciplining everyone – a King who is as powerful in Dover as in London – clan rule may be the best available alternative.[5]

The Rise of Policing and Lawyering

Robert Putnam's best-selling book *Bowling Alone* is famous for documenting the decline in US social networks. The title refers to the dramatic rise and fall of league bowling, and Putnam demonstrates similar trends for religious participation, trade unionism, parent–teacher associations, informal interaction with neighbors and friends, and many other forms of social networking. But the book also touches on the question: what comes instead of social ties? Putnam argues that the decline of networks brings about a demand for substitutes, such as police, lawyers, and judges. The decline in networks coincides with a sharp increase in policing and lawyering starting around 1970 (Putnam, 2000, Ch. 8). Here is Putnam's summary:

> Throughout the American society and economy, beginning around 1970, informal understandings no longer seemed adequate or prudent. [...] Spouses, neighbors, business partners and would-be partners, parents and children, pastors and parishioners, donors and recipients – all of us abruptly began to demand to "get it in writing."

In our formal model, the reduction in networking is best captured as a reduction of the interaction frequency δ, which in

---

[5] In terms of our model, collective responsibility would essentially act in the same way as increasing the continuation probability δ, but I refrain from spelling out the details.

turn may be causing a reduction in altruism α.[6] As we have seen above, reducing either δ or α makes it more difficult to sustain bilateral cooperation and thus increases the need for third-party enforcement of some kind.

[6] Again, Putnam (2000, Ch. 1) provides a striking illustration. He tells the story of Andy Boschma, a 33-year-old accountant who donates one of his kidneys to John Lambert, a 64-year-old retired employee of the University of Michigan hospital. Boschma is white, Lambert is black, and they know each other only because they have met regularly in the local bowling league.

13

Coercion: Costs and Benefits

Almost everyone agrees that professional enforcers are useful if they limit their activity to enforcing contracts. The vision of a Minimal State is precisely to guard private property and to uphold contracts. Where disagreement sets in is when the Enforcers take on the task of getting people to behave in ways they never agreed to. For example, people who subscribe to libertarian ideologies want to sharply limit the power of political authorities. Conservatives and social liberals accept that political authorities engage in redistribution and social insurance. Socialists and communists often want central authorities to go even further and direct substantial parts of production and consumption.

In this chapter, I present one argument for each side of this debate.

Exploitation

Not all relationships are mutually beneficial. Sometimes, large countries exploit small countries, powerful employers exploit powerless employees (slaves), and physically strong men exploit physically weaker spouses. Likewise, some political leaders and mafia bosses become more concerned with extracting large taxes and fees than with facilitating a sound business climate. The problem is that once their authority is respected, it is difficult to prevent them from abusing it. Just as the threat to inflict punishment can be used to sustain legitimate promises, it can be used for extortion.

In describing how the Danish vikings were able to extort more than 100 tonnes of silver from England during the 9th through 11th century, Rudyard Kipling in 1911 wrote the poem Dane-Geld. Two of the stanzas go:

> It is always a temptation for a rich and lazy nation,
> To puff and look important and to say: –
> "Though we know we should defeat you, we have not the
>   time to meet you.
> We will therefore pay you cash to go away."

> And that is called paying the Dane-geld;
> But we've proved it again and again,
> That if once you have paid him the Dane-geld
> You never get rid of the Dane.

To illustrate the logic as simply as possible, suppose each period Rowena can make a sacrifice for Colin's benefit. The sacrifice costs her 2 utils and yields Colin 1 util. Afterwards, Colin can inflict pain on Rowena. As before, ρ denotes the cost of inflicting punishment and π denotes the cost of being punished. Thus, each period has the following structure:

				NP	P
S	0,1			0,0	$-\pi, -\rho$
NS	2,0				

Stage 1   **Stage 2**

Figure 13.1   An Extortion game

Let $\pi > 2$ and $\rho < \delta/(1 - \delta)$. (As before, δ denotes the constant probability the game continues.) One equilibrium of this game is that (*NS*, *NP*) is played every period. But another equilibrium is that Rowena gives in to Colin's pressure, as follows:

- Stage 1: play *S* if always *S* or always *P* after *NS*; otherwise *NS*.
- Stage 2: play *P* if *NS* this period and never *NP* after *NS*; otherwise *NP*.

In other words, Colin threatens to inflict punishment in every period that Rowena does not make the sacrifice, and hence Rowena makes the sacrifice each period. Rowena clearly has nothing to gain by a one-period deviation, since the Stage 1 gain of 2 is outweighed by the immediate punishment $\pi > 2$. Why is Colin willing to punish? The logic should be familiar by now: If Colin does not punish, then Rowena will stop making sacrifices. Thus, he punishes if the following inequality is satisfied:

$$\delta + \delta^2 + \dots \geq \rho,$$

which holds if $\rho < \delta/(1 - \delta)$, which we have assumed.

For extortion to work, it is critical that Colin has real authority; he gets to choose the equilibrium. If Rowena could choose equilibrium, she would choose the strategy profile (*NS*, *NP*) every period regardless of history. At the end of Dane-Geld, Kipling advises Rowena to try to impose her preferred equilibrium:

It is wrong to put temptation in the path of any nation,
For fear they should succumb and go astray;
So when you are requested to pay up or be molested,
You will find it better policy to say: –

"We never pay any-one Dane-geld,
No matter how trifling the cost;
For the end of that game is oppression and shame,
And the nation that pays it is lost!"

To extort many people at once, it is also critical that subordinates are unable to coordinate their defections. If Colin has limited punishment ability each period, the subordinates could simultaneously fail to sacrifice, and Colin might be unable to punish all severely enough. In this sense, the model captures the insights of the maxims *divide and rule* (or *divide and conquer*) and *unity makes strength*. The former is the best advice to tyrannical rulers and the latter is the best advice to people who seek to resist tyranny.

Extortion is not a problem when rulers are benevolent. But even rulers who start out with admirable moral principles tend to become more selfish over time. In the famous words of John Dalberg-Acton, "Power tends to corrupt, and absolute power corrupts absolutely. Great men are almost always bad men ..."

While these observations justify checks and balances, they do not justify the view that rulers should never engage in coercion. There are sometimes sound reasons for coercing people to behave in ways that they do not want to, as we shall now see.

Desirable Taxation

In a hypothetical world where private property is perfectly protected and voluntary contracts are perfectly enforced,[1] would there be any need for a ruler to use additional coercion in order to bring about desirable cooperation?

In a famous article, Ronald Coase argued that the answer is no.[2] In particular, if there are no costs of writing and

---

[1] For concreteness, you may think of enforcement as a credible threat of harsh punishment in case of contract violation.

[2] The article is entitled *The Problem of Social Cost* and was published in 1960. It is worth emphasizing that Coase did not believe that the prerequisites are fulfilled in practice. To the contrary, he argued that we need to understand the ways in which they are not fulfilled to understand social institutions, including many aspects of the legal system.

enforcing contracts, two rational parties would always be able to voluntarily negotiate a mutually beneficial outcome. Coase's argument is generally accepted when there are two parties.[3] Let us call this the *Coase theorem.*

To illustrate Coase's logic with the help of game theory, consider the two-person social dilemma game of Figure 4.6. Let us allow the players to write a contract to play the efficient strategy profile (S, S). Specifically, let each player i promise to pay a penalty $\pi > 1$ to the opponent (player j) in case player i plays N. If they have written such a contract, the modified game is as depicted in Figure 13.2.

	S	N
S	2,2	$\pi, 3 - \pi$
N	$3 - \pi, \pi$	1,1

Figure 13.2   A social dilemma game with a penalty contract

Since $\pi > 1$, it is a dominant strategy for each player to play S. It is also clear why each player will voluntarily decide to sign such contracts if the player thinks that the opponent is signing; if she does not, she will each end up with 1 util instead of 2 utils.[4]

Food for Thought 13.1 *On December 12, 2020, Swedish newspaper* Expressen *printed an opinion piece authored by a young politician, My Pohl. She calls for a dismantling of the Swedish welfare state, as it is based on coercion rather than*

---

[3] The only reservation is that negotiators could attempt to use tough bargaining tactics to gain at the others' expense. For example, if each negotiator insists that she get more than half of the available surplus, and no negotiator can back down from their ultimatum offer, then the final outcome will be inefficient. I resist the temptation to review the detailed arguments here.

[4] If we were to model the process of proposing and signing contracts as part of the overall game, there would often be a Nash equilibrium in which no contract is proposed, since each player thinks the opponent will not be signing. However, if a contract proposal is binding for the proposer once the responder accepts, the contracting game might entail exclusively efficient equilibrium outcomes.

voluntary contracting: "It is a contract that I never agreed to." "It has been forced on me by the State." Similar arguments against the coercive power of governments have been made by many others, including author Ayn Rand and philosopher Robert Nozick. What do you think about this argument?

If there are more than two parties, Coase's argument is generally rejected. To understand why, consider the following Multilateral Sacrifice game. There are $n > 2$ players. Each player can either sacrifice (play S) or not sacrifice (play NS). Think of the sacrifice as a work effort. A sacrifice costs c utils and each play of S gives *each player* access to an additional amount of a *public good* worth v utils. This is why the Multilateral Sacrifice game is typically called a *public goods game*. A public good is a good for which there is *no rivalry in consumption*. One player's consumption does not reduce any other player's ability to consume. For example, a television program or a digital copy of a book are instances of public goods. If all players sacrifice, each player gets a net utility of $nv - c$.

The example considers an imaginary world where people can freely negotiate transfers to shift utility between themselves. Therefore, it is natural to define *social value* as the sum of their utilities. We assume $nv > c$, so that the social value of the sacrifice is positive (otherwise the public good is not worth having). We also assume $v < c$ (otherwise, the public good is so attractive that players do not need to negotiate). For reference, let us enumerate these two assumptions.

Assumption 1 *The parameters satisfy the inequalities* $v < c < nv$.

Clearly, then, if players were unable to write binding contracts, each player would unilaterally decide not to sacrifice; NS is a dominant strategy. But our assumption here is that the players *can* write binding contracts. Let a contract specify a distribution of (utility) transfers depending on which players play S at the sacrifice stage. Any contract must be voluntary in the sense that it is only valid if it is accepted by every player involved in non-zero transfers.

Suppose to begin with that all players must participate in negotiations. Then there are negotiation procedures such that everyone will agree to sacrifice. For example, let one of the players, the *proposer*, be picked to make a take-it-or-leave-it offer to the other players. If the offer is accepted by all, it is implemented – otherwise no contract is implemented. Then, this proposer might put forward a contract specifying that each participant plays S, and in addition pays (almost) $nv - c$ utils to the proposer. If all accept, each gets a utility slightly above $nv - c - (nv - c) = 0$, except the proposer who keeps (almost) all the surplus. If at least one player rejects, all get 0.

Does the example suggest that Coase's argument is true even when there are more than two players? It does not. The argument assumed each player *had to* participate in negotiations. That assumption directly contradicts Coase's premise that negotiations are voluntary. A proper analysis of the question must instead allow the players individually to decide whether to take part in the negotiations or not. That is, decisions should follow the timeline:

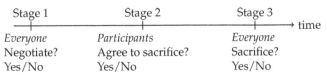

Figure 13.3 Timing

At Stage 1, each player decides whether to negotiate. At Stage 2, those players who decided to negotiate can write contracts between themselves. For example, this contract may stipulate that each of the participants in the negotiation makes a sacrifice, and that any participant failing to do so must pay a penalty to the other participants. At the third stage, everyone (whether they participated in negotiations or not) decides whether to contribute or not.

As always, to find a solution, we should start at the end of the game, that is, at Stage 3. Consider first what a player will do if the player did not participate in negotiation. Sacrificing costs c and yields an additional benefit $v < c$. Therefore, a non-negotiator will not sacrifice.

What about the negotiators' decision at Stage 2? In the spirit of Coase's claim that negotiations are efficient, let us assume that contracts maximize the total utility *of those players who participate in negotiations*.[5] Therefore, if there are m participants, they will reach an agreement that all of them should sacrifice if and only if $m^2v - mc > 0$. (Recall that each sacrifice creates a value v for everyone. Thus, the value of each sacrifice to the team of negotiators is mv.) Thus, the m negotiators will agree to all sacrifice if $m > c/v$ and not sacrifice if $m > c/v$.

Moving to Stage 1, we can then ask: What is the largest number of players m who would be willing to take part in contracting? Consider the utility of the contract participant with the smallest utility (who is hence most tempted not to take part in the negotiations).[6] This "marginal" participant's utility can not be greater than the average utility $mv - c$. What utility would the marginal participant obtain by refusing to negotiate? That depends on whether the remaining participants will be contracting to sacrifice or not. Suppose first that the remaining participants will be sacrificing. Since there are then $(m - 1)$ contributors, the utility of a "free-rider" becomes $(m - 1)v$. Thus, the marginal participant is willing to join only if

$$mv - c \geq (m - 1)v.$$

[5] For example, the contracts specify large penalties for failing to sacrifice after having promised to do so.

[6] If all participants are treated equally, pick one at random.

As you may readily check, this inequality holds only when $v \geq c$. That is, it never holds for the case we are interested in (Assumption 1 says $v < c$). In this example, nobody is willing to participate in negotiations if their participation is not decisive for a successful agreement!

Since the marginal participant is only willing to join when the negotiations otherwise fail (in which case the total sacrifice would be zero), the number of participants is the smallest m satisfying the inequality

$$mv - c \geq 0.$$

In other words, the number of participants is the smallest integer m such that $m \geq c/v$. That is, when n is large the number of participants is approximately

$$m^* = \frac{c}{v}.$$

The remaining $n - m^*$ players are *free-riders*.

Thus, when participation is voluntary, the utility of a participant is approximately

$$u_p = m^*v - c = 0,$$

and the utility of a non-participant is approximately

$$u_{np} = m^*v = c.$$

If, instead, contribution is compulsory, everyone would get utility $nv - c$. In other words, *compulsory sacrifice can make everyone better off*: When $nv - c > c$, even the potential free-riders would prefer that everyone is coerced.

This example confirms the conventional wisdom that it is desirable to have powerful governments that can coerce people to pay taxes, and that compulsory taxes are needed not only for the purpose of protecting property rights and uphold contracts, but also for the purpose of investing in public goods, such as roads, parks, and telecommunications. In the absence of coercion, voluntary contracting is insufficient to provide adequate amounts of public goods.

Food for Thought 13.2 *In their Nobel lectures December 8, 2018, both William Nordhaus and Paul Romer talked about policies to limit future emissions of carbon dioxide into the atmosphere. Nordhaus proposed to start climate clubs, where member countries commit to large emission reductions and also to impose large tariffs on non-members. (i) What is the logic of this proposal? Romer argued that an additional key to solving the climate problem lies in the moral improvement of individuals. (ii) What is the logic of this proposal?*

14

Contracts and Governance

In the rest of the book, I maintain as a basic assumption that a third party protects property rights and enforces contracts. We have established that frictionless contracting and enforcement allows two parties to attain efficient outcomes in this setting: When n is equal to two, the Coase theorem is true – it even rhymes. We shall now do what Coase impelled us to do, namely, investigate the obstacles ("transaction costs") that prevent fully efficient outcomes in practice.

As a backdrop to this exercise, I often think about a fascinating graphic in Bloom and van Reenen (2010). It depicts the distribution of firms' productivities in a variety of countries: While all the countries have some highly productive firms, poor countries also have a long tail of low-productivity firms. Arguably, the fundamental problem of development is to increase the share of highly productive firms. So let us now use the concepts we have established and try to identify some of the contracting frictions that may be responsible for low productivity.

To understand what separates a well-organized firm from a poorly organized firm, we need a language for discussing what firms do. Furthermore, in order to understand why poorly organized firms survive, we need to understand what prevents the well-organized firms from growing and taking over their resources. I address the first question in this chapter and the second question in the next chapter.

Some early literature on the theory of the firm tended to treat firms as centrally planned economies where coercion replaced voluntary market interaction. And it is true that the owners of a firm have more decision rights than the employees. Boards and CEOs are a bit like governments and prime ministers. However, in modern societies, slavery contracts are forbidden.[1] The manager cannot coerce the employee in the way that a government can impose taxes and other duties on citizens. A firm is more like a nexus of contracts, where participation is ultimately voluntary for everyone.

But if the firm is just a nexus of contracts, couldn't we just as well specify *everything* in a contract? Why do we need bosses to make decisions? And if we need bosses, why are they not also owners? Why does the modern corporation usually separate ownership and control?

Presumably, the reason why we set up elaborate governance structures is that detailed contracting doesn't work. For example, contracts may be impossible to enforce because enforcers can't verify what has happened, and hence whether anyone has violated the contract. This is called the *verifiability problem*. Alternatively, it is too costly to think through and write down all eventualities; the contracting process itself becomes an excessive burden.[2]

---

[1] In pre-modern societies, slavery was common. Landowners would frequently torture their workers as punishment for lax work. If you want to know the details – I am not sure you do – I can recommend a visit to one of Italy's five torture museums, in San Gimignano, Siena, Volterra, Lucca, or Montepulciano. In San Gimignano, if your stomach is not upset yet, you might as well visit the neighboring death-penalty museum.

[2] See Tirole (2009) for this argument, as well as a discussion of how the two issues are linked.

In this chapter I provide a brief introduction to the theory of contracts and governance, with a focus on responses to the verifiability problem.

Baseline: Verifiable Cash Flows and Profit Sharing

Rowena and Colin can each take an action, a_R and a_C respectively. Think about the actions as effort levels, which can take any non-negative value. Higher efforts increase revenues $r(a_R, a_C)$, which may in principle be shared in any proportion between Rowena and Colin. The cost of exerting effort falls on the person exerting it, so person i bears the cost $c_i(a_i)$. Letting α_i be i's share of the revenues, we assume utilities can be written

$$u_i(a_i, a_j) = a_i r(a_i, a_j) - c_i(a_i). \qquad (14.1)$$

That is, the costs are measured in monetary equivalents, and the players are risk neutral.

Suppose to start with that it is possible to contract directly on actions. Then, it is possible to divide the profits, call them

$$p(a_R, a_C) = r(a_R, a_C) - c_R(a_R) - c_C(a_C),$$

in any proportion between Rowena and Colin. Specifically, suppose the functions are such that there is a unique profit-maximizing action profile (a_R^*, a_C^*).[3] In this case, it is easy to implement the profile (a_R^*, a_C^*). To do so, simply write the following contract, where α is a constant strictly between 0 and 1:

---

[3] For example, the profit-maximizing action profile is unique if the revenue function is weakly concave and the cost functions are strictly convex, as this makes the profit function strictly concave.

The undersigned agree to take actions a_R^* and a_C^* respectively. If we do so, the resulting profit is to be split with a share α to Rowena and a share $(1 - \alpha)$ to Colin. If any party fails to take the stipulated action, that party should pay a penalty ρ to the other party. Signed, Rowena and Colin.

Clearly, if ρ is large enough, it is always better to take the agreed action than to violate the contract. Or to use our game theoretic vocabulary: Taking the agreed action is a *dominant strategy*.

What if the actions are unverifiable? As it turns out, verifiability of actions is not important at all! It is enough that all revenues and costs can be verified. In fact, even the large penalties may be superfluous. The simplest and most common contract can solve the problem. Specifically, suppose Rowena gets a fraction α of the profit and Colin gets a fraction $(1 - \alpha)$ of the profit, *no matter what they do*. We can then prove the following result: *Under a share contract, (a_R^*, a_C^*) is always a Nash equilibrium.*

The proof is straightforward. Suppose Rowena thinks Colin will take the action a_C^*. Then her problem is to maximize $\alpha p(a_R, a_C^*)$. The unique maximizer is thus a_R^*. (The positive parameter α is irrelevant for the maximization problem. Write down the first-order condition, or graph a numerical example, and you will see what I mean.)

Depending on the functional form of the revenue and cost functions, the share contract might even yield an equilibrium in dominant strategies. If you have ever solved an optimization problem by analyzing the first-order conditions, you can probably solve this exercise.

Exercise 14.1 *Suppose the revenue function is $r = a_R + a_C$ and the cost functions are $c_R = a_R^2/2$ and $a_C^2/2$. (i) Derive the profit maximizing actions. (ii) Show that these actions also constitute a dominant strategy equilibrium.*

To summarize, efficient contracting does not generally require that it is possible to verify actions directly. An accounting system that verifiably registers all revenues and costs may enable Rowena and Colin to cooperate perfectly by writing a simple share contract. Similarly, if Rowena and Colin are employees in an organization, they can be given a *team incentive* contract of this form.

Unverifiable Costs and Team Incentives

Often, the costs of producing something are non-monetary. For example, the cost may arise from spending time on mental activities. A lawyer spends much of the time reading and thinking. How can those costs be measured? Can an external party know whether the lawyer was analyzing a client's case or planning next week's substitutions for her Fantasy Premier League team?[4] Probably not. While the quality of the lawyer's advice might eventually materialize in the client's verifiable revenues, the actions and their costs will never be verifiable.

When both the actions and their costs are unverifiable, it is much trickier for Rowena and Colin to write a contract that provides correct incentives. Consider what happens if they write a simple share contract, giving Rowena a share α of the revenue and Colin the remainder. Formally, Rowena gets $w_i = \alpha r$. She thus maximizes

$$\alpha r(a_R, a_C) - c_R(a_R).$$

Her optimal action solves

$$\alpha \frac{\partial r(a_R, a_C)}{\partial a_R} - \frac{\partial c_R(a_R)}{\partial a_R} = 0$$

---

[4] If you don't know what FPL is, never mind – you get my point.

instead of

$$\frac{\partial r(a_R, a_C)}{\partial a_R} - \frac{\partial c_R(a_R)}{\partial a_R} = 0.$$

Set $\alpha = 1/2$. Using the revenue and cost functions from our example (Exercise 14.1), it follows that $a_R = 1/2$, which is only half the optimal level 1. Note that it does not matter what Colin does; $a_R = 1/2$ is a dominant strategy for Rowena.

Performing the same analysis for Colin yields $a_C = 1/2$. It follows that Rowena and Colin each get a utility of

$$\frac{1}{2} - \frac{1}{2}\left(\frac{1}{2}\right)^2 = \frac{3}{8}$$

instead of 1/2 which they would get in the efficient solution. They suffer because their costs are not being measured and hence cannot be contracted upon.

You might think that Rowena and Colin may write a smarter contract. For example, the share contract may additionally ask the Enforcer to punish them both – say by imposing a penalty ρ – in case the revenues r fall below the level $r(a_R^*, a_C^*)$.[5] However, this solution is not convincing. Suppose Colin cheats and puts in a bit less effort than agreed. Rather than calling on the Enforcer to punish them both, Rowena has an incentive to let bygones be bygones – to "settle out of court."

Holmström (1982) proposes a solution to this problem. He argues that Rowena and Colin need the help of a different third party, namely an Employer (owner). The Employer will keep track of the revenues and is more than happy to benefit (and report to the Enforcer if necessary) whenever Rowena's and Colin's joint performance is too low. According to this theory, the firm is essentially a credible collective incentive

---

[5] This penalty would be retained by the Enforcer. Letting one party pay the penalty to the other is a poor idea. If both pay an equally large penalty, the outcome is the same as if they pay no penalty at all.

mechanism (rather than a metering device that records actions or costs).[6]

Consider the following team incentive contract, where w_i denotes the compensation for employee i:

$$w_i = \begin{cases} r(a_R^*, a_C^*)/2 & \text{if } r \geq r(a_R^*, a_C^*); \\ -\rho & \text{otherwise.} \end{cases} \qquad (14.2)$$

That is, each of the two team members gets paid half of the revenue if the revenue target is reached and nothing otherwise. Often, the contract would be framed as a bonus for good performance rather than a penalty for bad performance, but that's semantics. For concreteness, let us put in the numbers from Example 14.1. There, $a_R^* = a_C^* = 1$, $r(a_R^*, a_C^*) = 2$, and $u_i = (a_R^*, a_C^*) = 1/2$. Thus, it is straightforward to prove that the efficient outcome (a_R^*, a_C^*) is a Nash equilibrium under the contract (14.2): If Colin plays $a_C = 1$, Rowena gets utility $u_R = 1/2$ if she plays $a_R = 1$, while she gets $u_R \leq -\rho$ if she plays $a_R < 1$. Playing $a_R > 1$ also yields $u_R < 1/2$, since costs are greater and compensation is the same. The same logic applies to Colin. So perhaps it doesn't matter that costs are unverifiable after all?

However, the efficient equilibrium under high-powered team incentives is typically not the only equilibrium. Suppose $\rho > 1$. Then even the extremely asymmetric actions $(0, 2)$ and $(2, 0)$ constitute Nash equilibria. To see this, suppose Rowena thinks that Colin puts in no effort. Then she has the choice between (i) effort $a_R = 2$, which gives her compensation of 1 and a cost of $(1/2)2^2 = 2$ for a net utility of -1, and (ii) effort 0, which gives utility $-\rho$ and thus is even worse. Due to the convex effort cost, asymmetric equilibria are unattractive.

---

[6] The discussion of team bonuses is relevant even if you are not interested in the fundamental issue of why there are firms, as target-based team bonuses are used in practice. For a broad survey of collective pay-for-performance compensation schemes, including team bonuses, see Nyberg et al. (2018). For a careful field experiment on target-based team bonuses, see Friebel et al. (2017).

The equilibrium (2, 0) produces utility 1 for Colin and −1 for Rowena, implying that total utility is only 0 (rather than 1, which is the utility associated with the symmetric equilibrium).

That is, a high-powered team incentive may have the effect of pushing one person to work excessively hard in order to reach the target while the other free-rides. Students might recognize this phenomenon from group assignments, where each group member gets the same grade based on the collective effort.[7]

You may ask: Are these additional equilibria really a problem? Can't Rowena and Colin simply agree to play the best symmetric equilibrium? The short answer is: Did you ever try to make sure that everyone did their fair share of the group work? The longer answer is to refer you back to Chapters 9 and 10. A major message from these chapters is that coordination on a desirable equilibrium is by no means guaranteed. If Rowena and Colin live in a culture where agreements are expected to be honored, such high-powered team incentives might have the intended effect. In other settings, high-powered team incentives can generate more problems than they solve, as some employees find ways to free-ride on the hard work of others.

Suppose a firm has the problem that one of its two employees, say Colin, is free-riding on the other. Colin may be able to uphold his advantage either through traditions or through communication. How can the firm rectify this problem? In essence, it must change the culture. One approach would be to undermine Colin's stronger position and hope Rowena and Colin themselves can establish a better equilibrium. But, as the game has a whole continuum of equilibria, relying on the

---

[7] Reducing the incentive p could help. As Rowena is no longer willing to do all the work to rescue the team bonus, Colin cannot shirk quite as much in any equilibrium. However, this solution has its own drawback. Whenever $p < 1$, complete free-riding ($a_R = a_C = 0$) is also an equilibrium. The smaller is p, the more the parties must trust each other to be willing to put in high effort.

employees to switch smoothly to a particular new equilibrium might be too optimistic.

An additional measure is to let the Employer take a more active role in coordinating the efforts, for example by telling the two employees that their efforts should be equal. But (as we discussed in Chapter 10), such use of formal authority will only work if the firm has already changed its culture; if the employees continue to view Colin's authority as more powerful than the Employer's, it will not matter what the Employer says. If the culture is dysfunctional and resistant to change, the target-based team bonus contract is less attractive. A simple share contract could be better.

Formal and Informal Contracts: Ownership vs Control

This chapter has been concerned with the role of formal contracts. In reality, many contracts are informal – both between firms and within them. If we want to understand why firms own assets rather than having the employees owning them, and if we also want to tell a plausible story about the role of managers, perhaps we need to pay attention to the legal and the relational dimensions simultaneously. The "relational theory of the firm" takes this perspective.

In the relational theory of the firm, actions, costs, and revenues are all unverifiable. The legal system only protects property rights to assets and enforces unconditional payment contracts. As in Chapter 11, the question is whether informal threats can deter cheating, but the focus is now on how asset ownership affects the severity of the punishment threat.

As an illustration, let me use relational arguments to explain the separation of ownership and control that characterizes the modern corporation. That is, corporations are typically owned by absentee investors, who themselves have no use for the assets, or are even blocked from using them.

Such companies were initially viewed with scepticism.[8] Yet, the prevalence of this corporate form suggests there are benefits.

I propose that the benefit of having absentee asset ownership is that managers and workers have stronger incentives to behave diligently when they are afraid of losing access to the assets. A truck driver is less productive without the truck. The skills of a loan officer are worth little without access to the bank's money.[9] When people can't bring the assets with them, they will be more careful to maintain their relationships.

Here is a simple formal version of the argument. Suppose Rowena and Colin are engaged in a joint project that requires access to a single asset. Every period, they each decide whether to work hard (W) or free-ride (F). Their payoffs are as in Figure 14.1. (Note that this is just the social dilemma game of Figure 4.6).

	W	F
W	2,2	0,3
F	3,0	1,1

Figure 14.1   Employees' stage game

Without access to the asset, each of them can earn at most some outside payoff o_I per period, where $1 < o_I < 2$. With

---

[8] Adam Smith (1776) writes:

> The directors of such companies ..., being the managers rather of other people's money than of their own, it cannot well be expected that they should watch over it with the same anxious vigilance with which the partners in a private co-partnery frequently watch over their own. Like the stewards of a rich man, they are apt to consider attention to small matters as not for their master's honor, and very easily give themselves a dispensation from having it. Negligence and profusion, therefore, must always prevail, more or less, in the management of the affairs of such a company. It is upon this account that joint stock companies for foreign trade have seldom been able to maintain the competition against private adventurers.
> (Book V, Ch. I, Part III, Art. I)

[9] Technically, bank deposits are liabilities not assets, but you know what I mean.

access to the asset, the asset owner can earn a higher outside payoff o_h, where $o_l < o_h < 2$. As in Chapter 11, the challenge is to sustain cooperation, i.e., to play (W, W) every period. The harshest threat is to end cooperation forever. Without the outside option, this threat would yield a per-period payoff of 1 to each. Now, the threat is to impose the outside option instead.

To fix ideas, let the asset be a saloon and suppose Colin and Rowena are the only people who can run the saloon and generate a per-period revenue greater than 2 (i.e., 1+1). If the cooperation falters, it is better for one of them to move to another town and earn o_l by working in a saloon there, while the other stays and earns o_h.

If either Rowena or Colin owns the saloon, cooperation can be sustained only if the asset owner is not tempted to make a one-step deviation and play F, i.e., if

$$2 + 2\delta + 2\delta^2 + \dots \geq 3 + o_h\delta + o_h\delta^2 + \dots$$

Using the same tricks as in Chapter 11, this expression reduces to

$$\delta \geq \frac{1}{3 - o_h} = \delta_h.$$

If neither Colin nor Rowena owns, the condition instead becomes

$$\delta \geq \frac{1}{3 - o_l} = \delta_l.$$

The idea is simple. If there is an outside owner of the saloon, and the trust between Rowena and Colin has been destroyed, their relationship ends, and the optimal arrangement is for one of them to take over the saloon. The owner thus sells the saloon to the highest bidder. Since Colin and Rowena are both willing to pay up to $(o_h - o_l)/(1 - \delta)$ – i.e., the net present value of operating the current saloon rather than a faraway saloon – this is the price the saloon will sell for. Thus, after a deviation, each of them earns the (equivalent of the) net present value associated with working in another town. Thus, if δ lies between δ_l and δ_h, cooperation can be sustained if there is an outside asset owner, but not if either Colin or Rowena owns.[10]

Outside ownership is most advantageous when the difference $o_h - o_l$ is large, that is when the asset is relationship-specific (o_h/o_l is large).[11]

Food for Thought 14.1 *In a famous study, Joskow (1985, 1987) describes relationships between coal mines and nearby coal-burning power plants. A major finding is that vertical integration between the mine and the power plant is more likely when such a pair is located far from other mines and plants. How would you modify the model above to capture this insight?*

Unverifiable Benefits: Control as a Bargaining Chip

In some cases, even revenues are unverifiable. In other cases, the benefits that efforts generate do not take the form of revenue at all. Sometimes, they are entirely non-monetary. In this case, a contract enforcer may find it impossible even to observe the benefits. As an example, consider the provision of elementary schooling. Here, the benefit is the education that the school provides.

---

[10] What if they own the saloon together? In that case, if trust breaks down, they must decide who will move and who will keep the saloon. A natural outcome is for one party to stay and pay the other $(o_h - o_l)/2$. Foreseeing this, each party has an incentive to deviate if $\delta < 1/(3 - o_m)$, where $o_m = (o_h + o_l)/2$. Thus, joint ownership is better than separate ownership, but not as good as outside ownership.

[11] In this simple model, there is no downside to outside ownership. However, it would be easy enough to introduce some. For example, suppose the asset will be sold when the relationship ends and that the sales price depends on some non-contractible maintenance activity by the users.

If neither benefits nor costs are verifiable to the enforcer, what use is there for enforceable contracts? The answer is that we can still contract about decision rights, such as the right to control assets. Indeed, protecting property rights is a prime function of legal authorities all over the world.

To fix ideas, let us stick with the schooling example.[12] Suppose the right to implement new practices in a school can be assigned either to the Headteacher or to the Public School Board. In the first case, we say the school is *private* (privately operated), and in the second case we say the school is *public* (publicly operated). Our question will be: What are the costs and benefits of private schools? However, as you will see, the framework lends itself to study many other problems concerning the optimal assignment of decision rights.

The major point I want you to take away from the upcoming discussion is that decision rights convey bargaining power and that bargaining power conveys incentives. Thus, decision rights ought to be – and in our simple setting will be – lodged with the people whose increased efforts are most socially beneficial. In the school example, you might think it is obvious that the Headteacher should have decision rights, because she is the one who can innovate. However, that depends on whether innovation is always a good thing. If innovations reduce costs but reduce quality even more, then it might be better that the Public School Board has the decision rights.

Here is the model. The Headteacher can exert effort to innovate. Denote the effort level a and let it take any nonnegative value. Suppose the Headteacher's cost of the innovation effort is also a. If the resulting innovation is implemented, the cost of delivering education changes by an amount $c(a)$ which may be positive or negative, depending on the nature of the innovation. The benefits are changed by an amount $b(a)$. If there is no innovation effort, or if the innovation is not implemented, $c(0) = b(0) = 0$.

---

[12] My analysis here builds on Hart, Shleifer, and Vishny (1997).

Before the Headteacher settles on the innovation effort, it is decided whether the school is privately or publicly controlled. If it is private, the Headteacher has the right to implement innovations unilaterally. If it is public, the School Board has the final say. It is impossible to verify the innovation effort a. However, once the innovation has been produced, it is possible to negotiate about its implementation. Let $t(a)$ denote the transfer from the School Board to the Headteacher. For simplicity, we assume the two parties neglect sunk cost when they bargain; morality plays no role. Instead, they split equally any gains from a successful negotiation (relative to the outcome if they fail to agree). Figure 14.2 displays the sequence of moves.

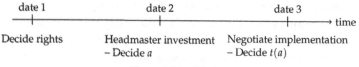

date 1	date 2	date 3
Decide rights	Headmaster investment – Decide a	Negotiate implementation – Decide $t(a)$

Figure 14.2   Timing

We consider two cases. In the first case, the innovation is a pure quality improvement. That is, raising a raises the benefit b but has no effect on the cost c. In the second case, the innovation is a cost reduction, which reduces c, but also reduces the benefit b. In each case, we study what happens under private and public ownership respectively.

Quality improvement

Had it been possible to contract on the quality-improving investment level, the Headteacher and the School Board would have chosen a to maximize $b(a) - a$. Assume there are decreasing marginal returns to quality improvement, i.e., $b''(a) < 0$. Then, the efficient investment solves the first-order condition $b'(a) - 1 = 0$. But, since the investment is not contractible, it will fall short of the efficient level, as we shall now see.

The first thing to notice is that the School Board will never refuse to implement an innovation that improves quality.

If the School Board owns, it will also have no reason to compensate the Headteacher for the improvement – as the Headteacher has nothing to bargain with. Since public ownership implies that the School Board will simply appropriate the innovation, the Headteacher has no incentive to innovate. That is, the equilibrium level of innovation is $a = 0$. Thus, the model picks up the idea that public ownership may stunt creativity.[13]

If, instead, the Headteacher owns, she can threaten to refuse implementation of the innovation. Therefore, the School Board will offer to pay half the benefit, i.e., $t(a) = b(a)/2$. Foreseeing this will be the outcome at date 3, at date 2 the Headteacher chooses innovation effort a to maximize $b(a)/2 - a$. In that case, the Headteacher's choice of quality level will solve the first-order condition $b'(a)/2 - 1 = 0$. That is, the investment under private ownership is given by the solution to $b'(a) = 2$, which yields a smaller investment a than the efficient level, which solves $b'(a) = 1$.[14] That's intuitive: The Headteacher only gets half the gain she creates but must bear the full investment cost. However, the private ownership outcome is considerably better than the public ownership outcome. The Headteacher is more willing to invest when she has more bargaining power and thus can earn a return on the investment.

Cost Reduction

Investment in cost reduction lowers costs but also lowers benefits. Let us focus on the case where c falls more than b, so that the innovation will eventually be worth implementing, i.e., $b(a) - c(a) > 0$.

---

[13] Many educators have other goals than earning money, so please don't see the analysis as an empirical claim that nobody innovates when the profit motive is absent. But as you can check for yourself, all the qualitative results hold even if the Headteacher is somewhat unselfish.

[14] If you are unsure, please draw the graph for $b(a)$, for example in the case $b(a) = a^{1/2}$ and consider the points where the slope is 2 and 1 respectively.

Under public ownership, the Headteacher has no rights. The School Board does not like the reduced quality. It will only agree to implement the innovation if the Headteacher pays for it. (In reality, the payment takes the form of reduced compensation to the private school.) The School Board will negotiate a compensation

$$t(a) = (b(0) - b(a)) + (b(a) - c(a))/2.$$

The first term compensates for the drop in quality and the second term is half of the gain the innovation generates. Thus, the Headteacher will make the investment a that maximizes

$$-t(a) - c(a) - a = (b(a) - c(a))/2 - a.$$

As in the case of quality improvement, the Headteacher underinvests, because she gets only half the benefit but must bear the whole investment cost.

Under private ownership, the Headteacher does not need to negotiate with the School Board. She unilaterally implements the cost reduction and gets all the gains from doing so. Thus, she chooses the investment a to maximize $-c(a) - c$. Since she neglects the negative externality in the form of reduced quality, she now *overinvests*.

To summarize, private ownership is desirable except when cost reductions precipitate large quality reductions. In this case, the underinvestment that public ownership entails may be preferable to the overinvestment that private ownership entails.[15]

---

[15] In reality, many other factors matter. In the school example, competition for pupils may temper overinvestment in cost reduction. Prison services constitute one area that seems uniquely poorly suited for privatization, since private owners are unlikely to be caring much for the prisoners and prisoners themselves have little choice. However, it is possible to verify some benefit measures – such as recidivism rates – so, with sufficiently smart regulation, perhaps the many private prison scandals will be a thing of the past. For an insightful survey of the experiences with private prisons around the world, see the Wikipedia article https://en.wikipedia.org/wiki/Private_prison.

Knutsson and Tyrefors (2022) use this theory to shed light on the quality of ambulance services in Stockholm, Sweden. There, private and public ambulances operate side-by-side and it is virtually random whether a mission is assigned to one or the other. Private ambulances perform well along contracted quality dimensions, such as response time. However, a larger fraction of the patients die. The reason is that private companies shirk on uncontractible service: Patients are classified as less severely injured and more often left at home. Also, private firms pay lower wages to their staff and offer worse working conditions. Hence, their workers have higher turnover.

Food for Thought 14.2 *Some Headteachers will be motivated by public service in addition to their own material benefits. How does this change the choice between private and public ownership? Does it matter whether the School Board has power over who gets to be Headteacher? What would happen if any privately owned school would have to be not-for-profit?*

15
Limited Liability and Corporate Finance

Why do poorly performing firms survive? That is, why don't market forces ensure that all the resources flow to the most productive firms? A leading explanation is that many firms become financially constrained; even when the firm is excellent, investors do not dare to let it have more resources.

When we study financial constraints, our starting point is typically that punishments are limited. For example, laws no longer allow creditors to inflict physical punishment on defaulting debtors, or even force the debtor to work as a slave (see Footnote 1 of Chapter 14). I should start by confessing that this is hardly the most fundamental friction in financial markets. In fact, it was to a large extent the market-place itself that came to prefer limited liability contracting. Nowadays, investors' claims are overwhelmingly on firms only, rather than on the firms' founders, despite the legal possibility of placing greater liability of founders, as was often done historically.

However, I will *not* try to explain why laws and market practices have changed away from unlimited liability and harsh punishments, which were common practices, even in the financially most developed countries, far into the

19th century.[1] Rather, I will merely explain the consequences of the kind of limited liability contracting that has emerged in their place.

The Ex Ante Diversion Problem

Consider an Entrepreneur (she), whose new project requires an investment of (fixed) size a.[2] The project delivers a (certain) verifiable revenue $r > a$. However, the Entrepreneur's own wealth is only $\omega < a$, so the Entrepreneur needs outside funds, say from an Investor (he). The problem, as seen from the Investor's point of view, is that the Entrepreneur cannot promise to execute the profitable project. Instead, the Entrepreneur might put the funds into a pet project. For simplicity, suppose the pet project doesn't generate any verifiable revenues at all. We assume for the moment that both the Entrepreneur and the Investor are completely selfish.

The pet project generates a private benefit b for the Entrepreneur, either in the form of enjoyment or in the form of future unverifiable revenues. To make the problem interesting, assume $\omega < b < a$. That is, the Entrepreneur would prefer executing the pet project to merely maintaining the net worth, but the pet project does not generate a positive social return.

---

[1] If I had to guess why legal punishments have become softer, I would venture that the legal limitations reflect the greater political power of poorer people, who are more likely to be debtors. If I had to guess why the market preference for limited liability corporations is so strong, I would venture that claims with more extensive liability would be too illiquid because market participants have more asymmetric information about the entrepreneur's financial situation than about the firm's financial situation. But other hypotheses also appear plausible. Note also that limited liability typically goes both ways: Just as the owner of a corporation is not personally responsible for the corporation's debt in case of bankruptcy, the corporation is not responsible for the owner's debt. This protection of firms' assets is known as entity shielding. I do not try to explain the benefits of entity shielding either.

[2] The exposition here builds extensively on Tirole (2001).

Of course, contracting would be easy if the Investor could credibly threaten to punish the Entrepreneur harshly in case she fails to deliver a positive rate of return on the investment. But, if the Entrepreneur's project is lodged in a firm with limited liability, harsh punishments are illegal. The Investor can extract verifiable revenues, or other assets owned by the firm, but they cannot extract unverifiable benefits or impose punishments.

To analyze this problem, it is helpful to consider the extensive form game, depicted in Figure 15.1.

In the figure, the Investor first decides whether to invest or not. Hence, we list the Investor's payoff first and the Entrepreneur's payoff second. If the Investor decides not to invest, the project does not get funded, and both parties get 0. If the Investor decides to provide the required funds, $a - \omega$, the Entrepreneur gets to choose whether to invest the money loyally or to instead put all the money into the pet project.

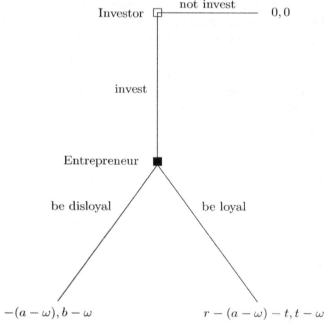

Figure 15.1 Financial contracting game I

If the Entrepreneur is disloyal, it does not matter what contract she has written with the Investor. Since the pet project does not create any verifiable returns, the Investor loses all the invested funds $a - \omega$, whereas the Entrepreneur makes a net gain of $b - \omega$. (These are the payoffs attached to the lower left branch.)

If the Entrepreneur is loyal, the contract matters. Suppose the contract specifies that the entrepreneur gets to keep an amount t, while the remaining revenue $r - t$ goes to the Investor. Thus, the Investor's net profit is $r - t - (a - \omega)$ and the Entrepreneur's net profit is $t - \omega$.

To see what will happen, we must find the subgame-perfect equilibrium. As usual, we start from the back. That is, we find out what the Entrepreneur will do if she gets the funds from the Investor. Try first yourself. Ready? The Entrepreneur will behave loyally if and only if $t - \omega \geq b - \omega$, or equivalently if $t \geq b$. That makes sense. The Entrepreneur's reward for being loyal must exceed the temptation to be disloyal.

Next, we find out what the investor will do. Investing and paying $t < b$ is meaningless, since the investment is a pure loss. Let us thus consider whether the Investor is willing to invest and let the Entrepreneur keep at least $t = b$. Investing is better if

$$r - b - (a - \omega) > 0,$$

or equivalently, if

$$r - b > a - \omega. \tag{15.1}$$

In other words, the revenue left after the Entrepreneur has been paid (the left-hand side) must exceed the amount of money the Investor needs to put in (the right-hand side). If the Entrepreneur's action had been contractible, there would have been investment whenever the return is positive, i.e., if $r \geq a$. Since $b > \omega$, the inequality (15.1) is more demanding. In other words, there can be projects satisfying $r > a$ which still do not get funding. The reason is that the Entrepreneur needs to earn a net profit of at least b in order to behave loyally.

The following observations are immediate:

1. Greater wealth ω can enable funding of socially valuable projects.
2. The same is true for anything that reduces b.

The first item offers a justification for the view that entrepreneurs should be allowed to retain business wealth, so as to be able to take advantage of investment opportunities. Financial markets are not so frictionless that penniless entrepreneurs with good ideas will always be able to raise all the necessary funds from outside investors.

The second item explains why it is often desirable to spend resources on monitoring the entrepreneur, keeping her from engaging in pet projects. It also explains why credit constrained entrepreneurs sometimes seek out investors who will threaten to punish her in case she fails to deliver – e.g., shadowy and ruthless moneylenders who inflict non-monetary pain if the debt is not paid in full. A more benign cause of a low b is that the Entrepreneur has high moral standards and would therefore not consider engaging in the unprofitable pet project to begin with; see Chapter 8. Yet another way to reduce b is to give the Entrepreneur inputs rather than cash. That is, the Entrepreneur can be funded by the suppliers through deliveries of goods and services that are useful for the project but have little value if diverted.

Can the Entrepreneur do anything more to secure funding for profitable projects? Yes, she could offer to sell some additional decision rights. For example, suppose she has some time that would normally be used for leisure or investment in human capital. By selling decision rights to a venture capitalist – who would then instruct her to spend time engaging with customers and engage in other activities that the entrepreneur feels uneasy with – she could raise more capital. Formally, the investors can force the entrepreneur to take an action at private non-monetary cost γ that yields a profit increase $\tau < \gamma$. Even if this action reduces the overall surplus, the Entrepreneur is willing to go along with it as long as (i) $r - b < a - \omega$, (ii) $r - b + \gamma > a - \omega$, and (iii) $b - \tau > 0$. That is, she is willing to sacrifice for the benefit of the investor if it is necessary to get the funds and if the pain is not greater than the pay she will get from the project.

The Ex Post Diversion Problem

Investors are not only worried that resources are diverted to undesirable projects. Perhaps an even greater worry is that the project returns are diverted. Here is a simple model of optimal contracts when the Entrepreneur can hold back some of the project revenues.

Suppose the Entrepreneur has no wealth. Crucially, the Entrepreneur can opportunistically retain all the revenues.[3] If this happens, the Investor may withhold the agreed compensation, but limited liability implies that the Investor cannot otherwise punish the Entrepreneur. Retaining the revenues is inefficient; for every dollar retained, the Entrepreneur gets to consume only $a < 1$ dollars.

Unlike the previous model, we now assume there is uncertainty about what the project returns will be. Let p be state of the world and let $r(p)$ be the associated revenues. The Entrepreneur is assumed to be risk averse; this is the only time in the book that I need this (realistic) assumption to make my point. The Investor is risk neutral.[4] The game thus looks as in Figure 15.2.

---

[3] It would be more realistic to assume that only some of the revenues can be retained, but the insights are the same and the present formulation is simpler.

[4] As usual in this literature, the assumptions are not meant literally to imply that entrepreneurs and investors have different degrees of risk aversion. Rather, they are a short-hand way of representing that the Entrepreneur has a large fraction of the wealth tied to the project, whereas the Investor is well diversified.

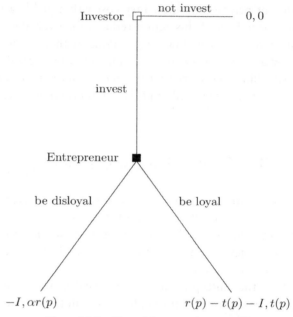

Figure 15.2   Financial contracting game II

The Entrepreneur behaves loyally in state p if and only if the compensation in that state, $t(p)$, (weakly) exceeds what she could retain, $\alpha r(p)$.

If the Investor has all the bargaining power, he should therefore give the Entrepreneur a contract that pays out exactly $t(p) = \alpha r(p)$. That is, he should offer the Entrepreneur compensation through shares in the project. Since the Entrepreneur has no wealth to invest, the Investor is willing to fund the project if

$$E_p\,[r(p) - t(p) - I] \geq 0.$$

Inserting $t(p) = \alpha r(p)$, the condition becomes

$$(1 - \alpha)E_p\,[r(p)] \geq I.$$

If the Entrepreneur has bargaining power (and the previous inequality holds strictly, so there is a surplus to be bargained about), a simple share contract is no longer optimal. The risk-averse Entrepreneur would want to increase compensation in the bad states. Thus, the optimal contract now is to have a flat wage w in combination with a stock option that comes "into the money" in the state where $w = ar(p)$. Just like the share contract, the stock options make sure that there is no diversion in the higher states.

Thus, this elementary model provides an explanation for why we see entrepreneurs being compensated either through stocks or through salaries and stock options.[5]

Food for Thought 15.1 *In his Nobel lecture of December 8, 2019, Abhijeet Banerjee presented evidence from several recent field experiments in which many randomly chosen poor individuals received a sizable increase in their wealth. Remarkably, these individuals tended to grow even richer over time. How would you explain this? (The lecture is available on nobelprize.org; the web page contains a huge amount of information about all the prizes, but you must dig to find it.)*

Food for Thought 15.2 *Abhijeet Banerjee has also coauthored an earlier observational study of agricultural productivity in India. The headline result is that productivity is higher in areas where the English colonizers gave land to poor farmers than in areas where they gave it to rich landlords. How would you explain that?*

---

[5] You might object that we get this result by making a strong assumption that the Entrepreneur is able to retain the same fraction of revenues irrespective of the state p. I think this assumption is less strong than it first seems. If revenues primarily vary because of the the price at which outputs can be sold, the assumption is that the Entrepreneur can withhold the same sales volume in each state.

16

Asymmetric Information

There is one more reason why rational people may fail to cooperate: They have different information. Two ideas are particularly important:

1. When you know something that I don't know, and I know that, I will try to prevent you from using your knowledge to take advantage of me.
2. When I know something that you do not know, and you know that, I will try to affect what you think I know.

Let us deal with these ideas in turn.

Screening

Suppose I have written a book you are willing to buy. After I have written the book, a copy is of no value to me. Before you have looked at the book, we both know you will be willing to pay either 20 dollars or 10 dollars for a copy of it. In fact, we know that with probability 4/5 you will be willing to pay 20 and with probability 1/5 you are only willing to pay 10 dollars. Let us assume that I can make a take-it-or-leave-it offer, and that I can do so before you have had a chance to look. I can also prevent you from looking before deciding.

My objective is to maximize my expected profit. What offer will I make to sell you a copy? Please stop and think before reading on.

Indeed, I will offer to sell the book for 18 dollars.[1] Since you are willing to pay 18 dollars, you will buy it. In this case, I have been able to grab the whole surplus. That's no surprise: We are only two people, information is symmetrically distributed, and contracts are enforceable. This is precisely the kind of case in which the Coase theorem (see Chapter 13) applies.

But suppose now that you have looked inside my book before making any decision whether to buy or not. You come to realize whether it is worth 20 dollars or 10 dollars to you. I do not have access to that information. What price should I set? Again, please think through the problem by yourself before reading on.

As you have probably figured out, I should set a price of 20 dollars. It is better to earn 20 dollars with probability 4/5 than to earn 10 dollars with certainty. But now, gains from trade are left on the table with probability 1/5. This is the core of the screening problem. I can find out how much you are willing to pay – that is, I can get you to reveal your type (i.e., screen you) – but the only way to do so is by giving up some of the potential gains from trade.

Clearly, selfishness is driving the efficiency loss. Altruism, fairness, or honesty could all eliminate it, as we shall now see.

Altruism: If I put a weight on your gains that is at least 3/4 of the weight that I put on mine, I would rather set a price of 10 than a price of 20. Non-profits frequently sell cheaply in order to fulfill their mission.

Fairness: If you would voluntarily pay me at least 8/9 of your privately known valuation, I would be better off than

---

[1] Well, probably I would sell for 17.99 just to be sure you do not decline the offer, but let us not be distracted by this detail.

by setting the price at 20. Pay-what-you-want pricing could in principle be profit-maximizing for the seller. Perhaps more often, it is a way for altruistic sellers to generate larger gains from trade and distribute them more evenly among buyers.[2]

Honesty: If I ask you how much you are willing to pay, and you are unable to tell a lie, then it becomes possible to set different prices depending on your willingness to pay. (If you find it easy to tell a lie, then I know what your answer will be: 10.)

Building relationships based on altruism, fairness, and honesty may overcome the screening problem. But how can you be sure someone is honest?

Analysis of the screening problem has generated large literature on optimal selling mechanisms. Given some goal (which could be maximizing expected utility for the seller or the buyer or some combination of the two) and some limitations (which could be the requirement that all participants are willing to take part in the transaction), what is the best way to conduct transactions? In the current case, i.e., a selfish seller transacting a single unit with a selfish buyer, whose valuation is private information and not connected to the seller's cost, the answer turns out to be simple. The best mechanism for the buyer is that the buyer gives a take-it-or-leave-it offer; likewise, the best mechanism for the seller is that the seller gives a take-it-or-leave-it offer.[3]

If, instead, the buyer is willing to buy multiple units, or if there are many potential buyers, the optimal mechanisms become more complex. With multiple units, the best mechanism for the seller usually involves quantity discounts; these have the

---

[2] A famous example of pay-what-you-want pricing is the band Radiohead's album *In Rainbows*. For more examples and some theoretical speculations, see Gneezy et al. (2012).

[3] It is not entirely trivial to prove which mechanism maximizes the seller's surplus. Intuitively, one might think the seller would want to put in place some kind of haggling mechanism, where there is trade with certainty if the buyer is willing to pay a high enough price, but trade with positive probability also if the buyer is only willing to pay a lower price. However, that intuition is wrong; see Riley and Zeckhauser (1983).

virtue of generating more trade with high-valuation buyers without forgoing all trade with low-valuation buyers. For example, mobile-phone operators often offer their customers a choice between a fixed subscription fee or pay-for-usage. The pay-for-usage price is much higher than the marginal cost of providing the service, and this might strike you as odd. However, the reason is simple: By making the pay-for-usage price unattractive to high-demand customers, the operators can raise the fixed fee they charge for the subscription contract.

With multiple buyers, the best mechanism for the seller is typically some sort of auction. Competition between the buyers then raises the price without the seller needing to worry that the item remains unsold (although it is typically optimal for the seller to put a price floor – a reserve price – to prevent the price from dropping too low).

There are many other applications of the general idea of using menus of contracts to exploit gains from trade between parties with different information. Firms can offer different tracks for their workers, schools can offer different tracks to their students, and industry regulators can offer menus of regulatory regimes to the firms they control.

Signaling

The signaling problem is related to the screening problem, but different. To fix ideas, consider the following example.

Signaling friendship. Person A wants to befriend person B. The value of the friendship, in the eyes of A, is either 1 or 2. Only A knows. Person B would like to befriend A if B's assessment of A's expected valuation of friendship is at least 1.5. However, B thinks a low value is more likely than a high value, and A knows this.

Person A can bring a gift to person B. Will there be a gift? If so, when and how large?

Please think through the question carefully before reading on.

What is the point of bringing a gift in this context? The point is to convince B that A is worth being friends with. Without any signal that A's value is high, B will not want to run the risk of being disappointed, since B's assessment of A's expected valuation is smaller than the required 1.5.

To convince B that A values friendship at 2 rather than 1, the gift must be large enough to overcome B's suspicion. That is, the gift must entail a sacrifice of at least 1 to A; only then will B be convinced A's friendship is worth having. In other words, the answer to the question is: *Yes, there will be a gift of at least 1 in case B's value is 2 and no gift otherwise.* The gift need not be much larger than 1 to constitute a credible signal. In fact, a gift of exactly 1 is what commonly accepted solution concepts imply.[4]

Note that the gift itself yields no utility. The possibility of sending a signal nonetheless creates a positive surplus. Person A makes a net gain of 1 util in case the value of friendship is 2, and Person B does not make a loss. However, positive surplus is not a general feature of signaling problems, as we shall see in the next example:

---

[4] The formal analysis of signaling games requires extensive notation, so I leave the mathematics aside here. Even the verbal description of the mathematical analysis can sound unbearably abstract, but here it is: Most solution concepts constitute refinements of Perfect Bayesian Equilibrium (PBE). A PBE requires (i) that each player optimizes given his own beliefs at each stage of the game, which is analogous to subgame-perfect Nash equilibrium that we described in Chapter 6, and (ii) that these beliefs satisfy Bayes' Rule whenever it applies, i.e., when players take actions that are not totally unexpected by the opponent(s). (I ask the forgiveness of first-year students; you may not have a course in statistics in elementary school, but if you don't know about Bayes' rule, it is worth your while to read up on it.) Refinements of PBE are assumptions about how beliefs are updated out of equilibrium, that is, after a player has done something the opponent didn't expect at all. Refinements have strange names, such as The Intuitive Criterion, D1, and Undefeated, all of which imply a gift of 1 by the high type in our example. (The two first refinements make this implication regardless of the likelihood that A has a high value of friendship. Undefeated implies no gift by anyone, and always friendship, if A's value is more likely to be 2 than 1.)

Signaling productivity. A worker faces a competitive labor market. (Meaning: the wage will be equal to the expected value of what the worker produces.) The worker's productivity, p, is either 1 or 2; productivity is privately known and cannot be costlessly revealed. Initially, employers think both productivities are equally likely. Both the employers and the worker are selfish and risk neutral materialists. The worker may try to signal productivity through education level e. The cost of education is e/p. How much education (i.e., what level of e) will a high-productivity worker take?

You might think there is not enough information to solve the problem, but there is. Let us break the problem down in pieces. (i) What would the wage be if there were no opportunity to take any education? Answer: 1.5. (ii) What would the wage be if the employers thought that the worker's productivity is 2 (respectively 1)? Answer: 2 (respectively 1). And finally:

Exercise 16.1 *How much education must a high-productivity worker take for a low-productivity worker not to be tempted to pretend to be a high-productivity worker?*

In this example, the opportunity for signaling is making nobody happier. The employers don't earn any profit anyway, the low-productivity worker loses a third of the wage, and the high-productivity worker's wage increase is eaten up by the cost of education, $e/2$.[5]

The notion that signaling opportunities could be harmful to the collective of senders seems to have been well understood for centuries. On October 21, 1314, Norwegian King, Håkon Magnusson (Håkon V), issued the following regulation:

---

[5] I am not here arguing that signaling is the primary function of education.

Many men use their clothing to show off and display their wealth. The behavior is of little use to this poor country and its inhabitants, and it is against the King's will. Therefore, it is forbidden to wear clothing that is composed of small pieces in different colors and so is all German fashion. Large metal pieces on the coat or on the headwear shall only be worn by females according to custom (...) the King wants everyone to wear the kind of dress that he himself wears. Anyone carrying different kinds of clothes shall pay a fine of [a substantial amount)].

Modern societies have put taxes on luxury goods for similar reasons.

Food for Thought 16.1 *Newly appointed central bank governors often take an early opportunity to raise the policy interest rate above the level that most economic experts think is optimal. Discuss this behavior in light of the logic of signaling theory.*

17
Application: The Oil-Pool Problem

We have been focusing on simple models. Reality is messy. As you apply the theory lessons to practical circumstances, your task will be to look at that messy reality and decide which lesson is most relevant. Sometimes, you may need more than one. Here is a brief illustration, building on field studies by Gary Libecap and Steven Wiggins.[1]

In the 1920s and 1930s, many landowners in the United States discovered that their properties were sitting on top of large pools of oil. The problem was that all the landowners sharing such an oil field had the right to establish wells and to extract oil from the same pool. The faster the extraction from a well, the more oil would flow beneath the well-owner's land, giving each landowner an incentive to build many wells and extract rapidly, at the expense of neighbors. Unfortunately, such rapid extraction was costly. More oil would get trapped and become hard to extract, and the greater extracted volume per time unit required greater investment in storage and transportation.

---

[1] See Libecap and Wiggins (1984, 1985) and Wiggins and Libecap (1985).

Let us pause there. Which model are you thinking of?
Exactly: The landowners face a social dilemma. We under-
stand that problem.

To avoid the economic waste, landowners were allowed
to contract with each other about the use of the lease. One
landowner could buy out the others (takeover), they could
establish a joint company (unitization), or they could have a
multilateral agreement regulating how much each owner was
allowed to extract (cartel).

Right, so contracting is possible and legal. There would
potentially be third-party enforcement. What problems are
then left? Well, landowners are not forced to negotiate with
each other – they could try to free ride on the contracting of
others – see the last part of Chapter 13.

The state of Texas imposed narrow limits on the landowners' right to arrange private cooperation. Contracting
was only allowed after discovery and full development of the
pool, and agreements were only legal if they were unanimous.
That is, all concerned landowners had to agree; otherwise,
there could be no cooperation at all. The state of Oklahoma
had similar rules but, instead of imposing unanimity, the state
imposed a 63 percent majority rule.[2] By contrast, the state of
Wyoming encouraged contracting of any kind already at the
exploration stage.

In Texas and Oklahoma, landowners often failed to agree,
especially when they were many and heterogeneous. For
example, at the East Texas oil pool, there were altogether
147 landowners who had a part in the field. They failed to
reach any private agreement. After seven months of stalled
negotiations, the state government intervened with regulations. However, the landowners even failed to respect these
regulations, except when the government arranged a military

---

[2] This might seem to be an unusual number, but supermajority rules often look
strange. For example, corporation takeover legislation often specifies that the
owner of 90 percent of the shares has the right to purchase the remaining
10 percent at a fair price.

occupation of the oil field. In Texas in 1950, twenty years after the development of these fields, only one percent of the output came from field-wide units.

In Wyoming, outcomes were better. By 1950 more than 60 percent of output came from field-wide units in Wyoming.

Note that the usefulness of regulations might be understood in light of our analysis in Chapter 13, which establishes the usefulness of coercion. But why were the problems so much smaller in Wyoming? Maybe because the landowners (leaseholders) were fewer and because they would have more symmetric information at the contracting stage? That would be consistent with our analysis in Chapter 16. But, since other things vary, it is difficult to be sure that asymmetric information was decisive.

In the context of an oil field, the problem of asymmetric information is that a leaseholder knows more about the value of being able to extract oil from her own plot of land, especially after she has already fully developed her wells. At the negotiation table, where it's being decided what share of total revenue should be assigned to which lease, everyone has an incentive to claim that their wells are particularly productive. If there are good reasons to think leases are similar, perhaps because nobody knows much about the exact location of the field yet, this might not be much of a problem. On the other hand, if some leases can reasonably be suspected of being at or beyond the boundary of the oil field, those leaseholders' claims might be met with suspicion.

This is the idea Libecap and Wiggins investigated. To make a long story short, they found that in places where negotiation took part after exploration and development, there was more disagreement involving leases with higher uncertainty, exactly as predicted by the asymmetric information argument.

Let me end by discussing a final disturbing fact that Libecap and Wiggins document: Both private agreements and state regulations divided up the right to income among claimholders according to how many wells they owned. At one level, this makes total sense: For example, the number of wells may be a sign of how much oil is located under the respective plot of land. However, if people anticipate that they will receive more revenue if they drill more wells, this again creates a social dilemma. Too many wells will be drilled.[3] In the messy reality cooperation sometimes succeeds, but if you look closely enough you may still find dimensions along which it fails.

[3] Incidentally, this is a problem in many industries that are operated by cartels. Members may be able to coordinate along some dimension, such as the price, but not along others, such as the capacity. Models of such semi-collusion have been used to explain the behavior of cement producers and airlines, for example.

18
Conclusion

We have studied how societies can avoid the destructive "war of all against all" and instead grow peaceful and prosperous.

The first pillar of a prosperous society is people's willingness to sacrifice their own interest for the benefit of others, either out of kindness or out of duty. While kindness is purely voluntary, duty is best seen as a form of coercion. Our conscience acts as an inner police force that compels us to take actions for the common good. Societies nurture the sense of duty through schooling, religious training, cultural activities, and governmental campaigns.

Schools are particularly important when people's cultural backgrounds differ, for example due to migration. North America provides a good example. There, many states adopted compulsory schooling laws as a nation-building tool to instil civic values into masses of culturally diverse migrants, who arrived during the "Age of Mass Migration" between 1850 and 1914 (as documented by Bandiera et al., 2019).

When instilling civic values, a central issue is to define the society to which loyalty is owed. Is loyalty owed to everyone or only to a more narrowly defined group? In the American example, racial segregation has implied that loyalty in part depended on skin color. In clan-based societies, loyalty to members of one's own clan can be strong, but loyalty to outsiders is typically weak. Willingness to sacrifice for the benefit of strangers seems to be strongest in countries that have nurtured a universalistic morality. It is these countries where the largest number of wallets are returned in the "lost-wallet" experiment.

The second pillar of a prosperous society is the ability to cooperate voluntarily. Cooperation requires a reliable shared memory of past events. Reading and writing in a common language facilitates such memories, as does accounting and public registries. Impartial legal systems help to ensure that self-serving biases are kept in check. Complex contracting is only feasible in societies where many people are well educated.

However, even under these circumstances, cooperation can be difficult. In Chapter 1, I mentioned Putnam's (1993) study of local governance in Italy. In the 1970s Italy devolved substantial powers to regional governments. The formal rules were essentially the same everywhere. Yet, they didn't work the same way everywhere. In some places, other rules took precedence. For example, Putnam (p. 5) recalls an episode in which a clerk responds to his nominal superior: "You can't give me orders! I'm 'well-protected'." In other places, the new rules may not conflict with old rules, but individuals find it unprofitable to comply with them since others don't.

Funding of desirable public goods often requires coercion. Therefore, the third and final pillar of a prosperous society is the ability to coerce individuals and firms to comply with social goals. The challenge is to endow governments with enough power to stifle theft and tax fraud, yet not so much power as to be unaccountable to the wider society. Public bandits are little better than private bandits.

19

More Food for Thought

In this chapter I have collected additional questions you may try to think about with the help of the concepts in the book.

Food for Thought 19.1 *During the 100-day period from April 7 to mid-July 1994, supporters of the Hutu majority government killed an estimated 500,000 to 1,000,000 Rwandans from other ethnic groups, especially the Tutsi. Research has shown that mass media played an important role in this genocide. For example, the radio station Radio Télévision Libre des Mille Collines (RTLM) led the propaganda efforts by broadcasting inflammatory messages calling for the extermination of the Tutsi minority, and killings were more extensive in regions reached by this station as well as in neighboring regions. (i) How can we explain the direct impact of propaganda on violent behavior? (ii) How can we explain the indirect impact, that is, the effect on people who were not themselves exposed to the propaganda?*

Food for Thought 19.2 *In his book* Power and Prosperity, *political scientist Mancur Olson distinguishes between the economic effects of different types of government, in* *particular, tyranny, anarchy, and democracy. Olson argues that under anarchy, a "roving bandit" only has the incentive to steal and destroy, while a "stationary bandit" – a tyrant – has an incentive to encourage some degree of economic success. (i) Please discuss whether tyranny is always preferable to anarchy. (ii) Please discuss what are the pros and cons of democracy relative to tyranny.*

Food for Thought 19.3 *Economist Paul Collier has written the following about corruption in the British Civil Service in the 19th century:*

Until well into the 19th century, the British public sector was very corrupt. Positions were bought and sold and contracts were awarded in return for bribes. Crises such as military humiliation in the Crimean War helped to shock governments into change. Opportunities for corruption were curtailed: recruitment and promotion were opened to competitive examinations. A new purposive ethic was promoted and serving the nation became the pinnacle of social prestige and self-worth. By the late 19th century, the British Civil Service had become honest and competent.

(i) How would you relate these strategies to concepts in the book? (ii) In view of the British success, why do not all countries have non-corrupt public sectors by now?

Food for Thought 19.4 *The location of industries across countries are almost certainly affected by differences in legal systems. In particular, industries that are dependent on large amounts of external investment tend to locate in countries with better legal systems. How would you explain this?*

Food for Thought 19.5 *In the early 1980s there was a remarkable turnaround of the airline SAS, from being one of the least* *punctual to being one of the most punctual airlines in the world. Asked how he had engineered this remarkable feat, the CEO Jan Carlzon often emphasized the building of a new and improved corporate culture. Please think about what those changes might have been.*

20
Further Reading

If you are interested in learning more, I here provide some references to get you started. Whenever possible, I point to a few core contributions as well as a recent survey. I also immodestly mention my own related work (please forgive).

Formalization is usually recent, and hence easy to trace. It is more difficult to identify the origin of the substantive ideas, as many of them were first expressed verbally. Much of the time I do not try to establish precedence with respect to substance. For example, the book touches on several ideas that occupied the founders of sociology, especially Durkheim (1893, 1900) and Weber (1905), but without relating directly to their work, which itself frequently has deep historical roots. For those interested in the history of sociological thought, including many topics I ignore, I refer to Nisbet (1993).

Cyert and March (1963) spearheaded sociologically informed studies of organization. Some of their ideas are now part of the formal literature, but many ideas remain informal. Maybe some advanced readers will be inspired to participate in the formalization of this fascinating field?

Chapter 1. The Organizational Challenge

There is a vast literature on why some countries fail and others succeed. The quantitative literature on the role of institutions and culture in the creation of prosperity is recent. The main challenge is to move beyond correlations to say something about causal relationships. Some recent surveys are Acemoglu, Gallego, and Robinson (2014), Alesina and Giuliano (2015), and Restuccia and Rogerson (2017); see also the books by Acemoglu and Robinson (2012) and Besley and Persson (2011). However, it is easier to discuss this empirical literature after we have introduced more theoretical concepts.

Psychologists come at these questions from another end. What are the fundamental mechanisms that allow people to get along? Can we understand what goes on in people's minds in social situations? Van Dijk and de Dreu (2021) is a recent survey of experimental work along these lines. Fehr (2018) discusses how these psychological mechanisms allow us to better understand corporate (and country) cultures.

Chapter 2. Sacrifice

The literature on social dilemma experiments is enormous. Deutsch (1958) demonstrates that behavior in Prisoners' Dilemmas is highly sensitive to instructions, for example whether subjects are instructed to behave competitively, individualistically, or cooperatively; see Sally (1995) for a survey of early experiments and Chaudhury (2011) for a survey of the period 1995–2010.

The literature on one-sided sacrifice, in the form of Dictator experiments, starts with a classroom experiment reported by Kahneman, Knetsch, and Thaler (1986). Engel (2011) surveys the early evidence. Grech and Nax (2020) observe that many of the experiments that ostensibly study one-sided sacrifice really study multi-sided sacrifice.

My own contributions to these experimental literatures are to demonstrate that verbal feedback serves to increase sacrifices in Dictator situations (Ellingsen and Johannesson, 2008a), and to investigate why social context in the form of labeling has considerable impact in Prisoners' Dilemmas (Ellingsen et al., 2012, 2013), but little impact in Dictator situations (Dreber et al., 2013).

Chapter 3. Selfishness, Rationality, and Utility

The basic foundations of choice theory were essentially complete by the mid-1950s, and some of this material can be found in any textbook in microeconomics. Utility theory was also the first topic that I spent years of my life digging into. In composing my literature survey, Ellingsen (1994), I learned that the topic is deep and fascinating, and that many economists are still confused about what it means to measure something. (Meaningful measures are defined by the measurement procedure.) I also decided never to write another survey.

Already Edgeworth (1881) provided a formal model of altruistic preferences. By contrast, the literature is less settled when it comes to modeling dutiful behavior. The approach that I take is inspired by López-Pérez (2008), DellaVigna, List and Malmendier (2012), Krupka and Weber (2013), as well as a close reading of moral philosophers such as Cicero (44 BCE), Hume (1751), and Smith (1759). Like them, I think that sacrifice is frequently involuntary – that is, dutiful rather than emphatic. Systematic evidence for this position is just beginning to accumulate. The pioneering modern laboratory experiments are due to Dana, Cain, and Dawes (2006) and Dana, Weber, and Kuang (2007) and the pioneering field experiments are DellaVigna, List, and Malmendier (2012) and Andreoni, Rao, and Trachtman (2017). My own experimental contribution is Broberg, Ellingsen, and Johannesson (2007). For a detailed discussion as well as my preferred formal model, see Ellingsen and Mohlin (2022).

More generally, we need to articulate formally the logic of appropriateness alongside the logic of consequences, as March and Olsen (1989) suggested that we should; see the plea in March (1994, Ch. 2). Versions of Equation 3.1 are bound to become more frequent in economic and social research. For example, this kind of utility function is required to express how legitimacy affects behavior in the framework of Greif and Rubin (2022) (although legitimacy could also affect behavior without impacting preferences, as we discuss in Chapter 10). It is also needed to express how people's loyalties depend on their social identities. For some contributions to social identity theory and applications, see Tajfel and Turner (1979), Akerlof and Kranton (2000), and Shayo (2009). Other insightful models of social values and norms include Brekke, Kverndokk, and Nyborg (2003), Bicchieri (2005), and López-Pérez (2008).

Frank (1988) provides an accessible account of evolutionary mechanisms, which are quite different from the cultural transmission alluded to above that may have shaped our preferences, updating Darwin (1871). If, instead, you want to become an evolutionary game theorist, the place to start is Weibull (1995). A fascinating recent contribution to the evolutionary theory of morality is Alger and Weibull (2013).

Chapter 4. Situations, Games, and Cooperation

Camerer (2003) remains the standard reference for behavioral game theory. Shafir and Tversky (1992) study experimentally the role of magical reasoning in sustaining cooperation, but the idea has been around for much longer.

As noted, we had a formal model of altruistic preferences already by the 1880s. In the 1960s, aversion to unfavorable inequality was discussed in half-formal ways under the umbrella of *equity theory*; see, e.g., Adams (1963). Formal models are due to Kirchsteiger (1994), Fehr and Schmidt (1999), and Bolton and Ockenfels (2000).

Seminal references to the experimental literature on self-serving bias are given in the text.[1] An early model of self-serving bias in the context of internalized norms is due to Rabin (1994). A formal model of strategic interaction between agents with over-optimistic beliefs is due to Yildiz (2003); see Yildiz (2011) for an overview of applications.

More recently, a lively research agenda is to understand how people manipulate their own beliefs, for example by avoiding information; see Dana, Weber, and Kuang (2007) for an original experiment and Bénabou R. and Tirole J. (2016) and Golman, Hagmann, and Loewenstein (2017) for surveys.

Chapter 5. Shared Understandings and Values

The literatures on culture, institutions, and norms go so far back in time and are so extensive that there will be many oversights for every single mention. After David Hume and Adam Smith, the analyses of Emile Durkheim and Max Weber have stood the test of time particularly well.

My definition of culture as comprising shared understandings and values is well in line with mainstream sociology. It follows naturally that institutions – the rules – tend to be shaped by culture; see Harrison (2000).

There is not yet a canonical *formal* framework of culture and institutions, but the next chapter sketches one. While it sometimes differs in minor details, my sketch is broadly compatible with informal definitions by economic historians, such as North (1991) and Mokyr (2016) or political scientists such as Ostrom (2000).

The measurement of cultural values used to be the domain of anthropologists (e.g., Murdock, 1967), but in the early

---

[1] My own little contribution is Ellingsen and Johannesson (2005).

1970s psychologist Geert Hofstede develops an influential measure of individualism (vs collectivism); see Hofstede (1980). For example, people are classified as individualistic when they are concerned with having an interesting job and with having time to spend as they wish, as opposed to having a secure job that is well respected among friends and family.[2] However, Hofstede is not convinced that culture is a deep determinant of economic performance. While he recognizes the strong empirical correlation between national income and individualism, he argues that the main causal effect runs from income to culture rather than the other way around (a position that he maintains for a long time; see, e.g., Hofstede, 2001, pp. 252–253). There surely is such an effect of economic prosperity on values, as documented by Inglehart (2018), for example, but the effect of culture on economic prosperity is of greater interest, at least to this book.

Krupka and Weber (2013) propose a general mechanism for eliciting social values: Ask people to guess how others will assess the appropriateness of each action and pay them for good guesses.

The game theoretic literature that uses culture to explain economic outcomes starts with Greif (1993, 1994).[3] Greif emphasizes what I call understandings and beliefs (and Greif calls cultural beliefs), largely leaving aside cultural differences in values. Appreciating Greif's contributions requires an understanding of indefinitely repeated games, which we cover in Chapters 11 and 12.

Another noteworthy theoretical contribution is Bisin and Verdier (2001), who offer a formal framework for studying

---

[2] There are other related concepts, such as the self-expression values that are extracted from the World Values Survey. However, this concept does not separate values from understandings, expectations, or even actions. For example, a person scores higher on the self-expression scale when the person has engaged in recycling to protect the environment.

[3] Another early contribution along similar lines is Greif, Milgrom, and Weingast (1994).

cultural transmission of preferences, with a particular focus on parents' incentives to shape their children's goals.

Modern quantitative work on culture starts with Putnam (1993) (which is partly based on Putnam's prior work with Robert Leonardi and Raffaella Nanetti). Putnam observes that national democratic reforms work much better in some Italian provinces than in others. With the help of regression analysis and informal reasoning, he argues that differences in prosociality and trust are the prime candidates for explaining why. He also argues that these differences in civicness explain difference in economic performance, and searches for the deep historical roots of civicness. Thus, Putnam's relatively quantitative analysis emphasizes the values side of culture.

At around the same time, Mauro (1995) introduces ethno-linguistic fractionalization as a deep cultural variable, demonstrating that it is closely linked to corruption, which is in turn linked to economic performance. In terms of our classification scheme in Figure 5.1, it seems plausible that fractionalization causes heterogeneous understandings and values, which in turn makes cooperation difficult. But, since fractionalization does not distinguish "good" and "bad" cultures, it largely fails to account for the regularities that Putnam observed.

The subsequent wave of quantitative research primarily shows *that* culture matters rather than providing precise reasons *why* it matters. Hall and Jones (1999) take as their starting point that economically productive culture is Western culture, and La Porta et al. (1999) link economic and other desirable outcomes to broad religions and legal systems. Putterman and Weil (2010) demonstrate on a large scale how culture moves with people; when considering the ability of early development indicators to predict current GDP, the history of a population's ancestors adds considerable explanatory power to the history of the place they live today. Institutions inhabit our brains rather than our real estate.

In the meantime, Acemoglu, Johnson, and Robinson (2001) bypass the cultural issue and focus directly on the institutions: Their idea is that Western colonialists have implemented their own institutions in places where they settle, but have implemented more extractive and less benign institutions in places that are not desirable for settling. This approach echoes Mauro (1995) more than Putnam (1993).

But gradually, researchers' focus has been returning to the specific links between culture and prosperity, as detailed in the survey by Alesina and Giuliano (2015). The role of generalized morality for well-functioning institutions is first investigated quantitatively by Tabellini (2008, 2010), whereas the negative relationship between kinship-orientation and generalized morality is emphasized by Greif and Tabellini (2010) in their comparison of China and Europe. Recent quantitative analysis of the impact of kinship-orientation on political and economic outcomes is due to Schulz (2022) and Bahrami-Rad et al. (2022); see also Enke (2019) and Schulz et al. (2019). For a broader perspective on cultural determinants of economic and political outcomes, see Henrich (2020).

As Restuccia and Rogerson (2017) point out in their survey, the literature on country prosperity overlaps significantly with the literature on the success of firms, which we touch on in Chapters 15 and 16.

Chapter 6. Predicting Behavior in Games

As mentioned in the text, John von Neumann and Oskar Morgenstern (1947) laid the foundation for modern game theory by their invention of expected utility theory, and John Nash (1950) proved the key theorem that all finite games have an equilibrium point. In his brief doctoral dissertation, together with his work on bargaining in Nash (1953), he also had the vision of non-cooperative game theory ("the Nash Program") that has come through today.

		Smallest choice						
		7	6	5	4	3	2	1
	7	13	11	9	7	5	3	1
	6		10	10	8	6	4	2
Your	5			9	9	7	5	3
choice	4				8	8	6	4
	3					7	7	5
	2						6	6
	1							5

Figure 20.1 The Blame game

There are many excellent texts on game theory. With the notable exception of Camerer (2003), most of them will take preferences for granted and focus on solution concepts involving rational beliefs. An elementary textbook is Dixit, Skeath and Reiley (2021). A fully rigorous text is Myerson (1991). An encyclopaedic text is Fudenberg and Tirole (1991). A good compromise between all of these is Osborne and Rubinstein (1994), which is rigorous yet accessible to the patient reader. If instead you want to have an entertaining book with tons of examples and hardly any math, you will enjoy Dixit and Nalebuff (2010).

Nash equilibrium is not always the best solution concept, however. Especially when people are inexperienced, they tend to have systematically incorrect expectations about what others will do. For predictive purposes, other models of players' beliefs sometimes do better, especially when players are inexperienced.

A famous and fun example of non-equilibrium beliefs occurs in the Guessing game mentioned in the text. Nagel, Büren, and Frank (2017) is a fascinating read about the history of the game (I make an appearance on the fringes). A less famous example is the Blame game of Ellingsen and Östling (2011). It makes for a good classroom experiment and runs as follows: Each student picks a number (an integer) from 1 to 7. A student's utility is determined by the own number and the lowest number picked, according to Figure 20. For example, if the own number is 4 and the lowest number is 2, then the player's payoff is 6. The game's unique Nash equilibrium is all players choosing 7. However, in a class of more than 20 students, the normal outcome is that some players choose 2, which means that the best number to choose is 3. Only as the game is repeated multiple times do people gradually converge on 7. Usually, nobody plays the dominated strategy 1. However, not everybody notices that if nobody picks 1, it does not make sense to play 2...and so on.

Chapter 7. A Model of Anarchy

A contest is a competition where participants need to pay even if they do not win, which is typical of wars, strikes, and sport contests, for example. The analogy between contest models and anarchy is by now commonplace (Skaperdas, 2006).

The model that I present is a so-called perfectly discriminating contest. According to the literature survey by Garfinkel and Skaperdas (2007), Trygve Haavelmo (1954) was the first economist to model the basic choice between production and appropriation. Gordon Tullock and Jack Hirshleifer have both had a great impact on this literature.

Some of my first work, Ellingsen (1991, 1997a), was on contests.

For an example of how contest models and other models of costly conflict shape the thinking about practical problems, see the survey by Blattman and Miguel (2010) of the literature about civil war.

Chapter 8. Changing the Game

To capture rigorously the notion that a player can change the game, one needs to start out with a description of players' awareness, and to let that awareness be asymmetric. The relevant game theory is quite recent; see Schipper (2014) for a brief review. I hope that most of my less rigorous analysis will prove correct even when done right.

Principles of unselfish (or "intrinsic") reciprocity are old, but systematic research only started a few decades ago. A recent experimental literature has made progress disentangling people's motives for punishing as well as rewarding others. Important early experiments were the ultimatum experiments of Güth, Schmittberger, and Schwarze (1982) and the trust experiments of Berg, Dickhaut, and McCabe (1995). For clean outlines of central issues, see Falk, Fehr, and Fischbacher (2003, 2008) and Cox, Kerschbamer, and Neururer (2016).

Could cultural values affect prosperity by affecting reciprocity? Social psychologist Yamagishi (1988) was the first to discover the (at first sight surprising) positive relationship between individualism and trust. The relationship between trust and economic performance that we saw in Chapter 1 as emphasized already by Mill (1848) was first documented rigorously by Knack and Keefer (1997). It seems likely that much of what appears to be positive reciprocity is simply a variant of generalized morality, which we have already discussed in (the notes to) Chapter 5.

As mentioned in the notes to Chapter 3, Frank (1988) discusses mechanisms that may have shaped our preferences. He particularly emphasizes the value of commitment to behaving reciprocally. One problem is that the second mover's reciprocal preferences are not directly visible to the first mover. Instead, commitment needs to be conveyed through costly signals. For example, Silverman (2004) demonstrates theoretically that the value of a reputation for being willing to use violence can justify otherwise pointless crime among young people in poor neighborhoods. For a brief introduction to signaling models, see Chapter 16 and the associated notes.

Formal models of unselfish reciprocity are new and often deviate from the standard assumptions of game theory by letting players care about the preferences or the beliefs of their opponents (see Sobel, 2005, for an overview). I tend to prefer the more conventional approach, which models reciprocity as a change in the weight put on another player's payoff in response to the (actual and potential) material payoff consequences of previous actions by that player. Examples of this approach are Cox, Friedman, and Gjerstad (2007) and Malmendier and Schmidt (2017); see also Charness and Rabin (2002, Appendix).

While practitioners have always relied on honor and handshakes for solving contractual problems, these mechanisms have played a relatively modest role in modern legal scholarship. Important exceptions are Macaulay (1963) and Macneil (1983). Macneil's emphasis on the contracting parties' values, both their loyalty and their reciprocity, is particularly relevant here. For a recent contribution to this literature, pointing to the possibility of promoting loyal sentiments through the formal contract itself, see Frydlinger and Hart (2020).

In the economic and psychological literature, reciprocity has long been important for the understanding of labor relations, where the notion that unfair pay could lead to reduced worker motivation has been gradually refined. An early statement is Adams and Rosenbaum (1962). Akerlof (1982) is an early formal model of gift exchange among employers and employees, and Fehr, Kirchsteiger, and Riedl (1993) is a seminal laboratory experiment. In the theory of the firm, reciprocity has played a more central role after the work on contracts as reference points by Hart and Moore (2008). Hart and Holmström (2010) use this idea to shed light on the role of organizational boundaries. (I have used it in my own work too; see Ellingsen and Kristiansen, 2022.)

The modern literature on why people keep promises began in social psychology; see, e.g., Loomis (1959). Much interest focused on the ability of people to use promises in order to cooperate in social dilemmas; see, e.g., Ostrom, Walker, and Gardner (1992) and the review in Sally (1995). More recently, behavioral economists have conducted new kinds of promise experiments. As mentioned in the text, I find Vanberg (2008) and Krupka, Leider, and Jiang (2016) particularly interesting.

My own contribution to the literature on promises is Ellingsen and Johannesson (2004b).

Thomas Schelling (1956) started the literature on credible commitments in bargaining, and Crawford (1982) made the first fully formal analysis of Schelling's idea that competition to establish commitment could lead to conflict. Ellingsen and Miettinen (2008, 2014), and Deb and Basak (2020) are more recent extensions and refinements.[4]

Chapter 9. Coordination

Coordination sometimes happens without any conscious planning, with individuals learning from their own and others' behavior. Kandori, Mailath, and Rob (1993) and Young (1993) are seminal contributors to the theoretical analysis of long-run coordination in games with several Nash equilibria. Among other things, the analysis predicts that risk-dominant equilibria are more stable than efficient equilibria in Stag Hunt (to the extent that the efficient equilibrium is not also risk-dominant). For an advanced textbook treatment of these issues, see Weibull (1995).

The question of conscious coordination is central in Schelling (1960). Farrell (1988) and Rabin (1990) study the use of communication for the purpose of coordination in games with complete information. Crawford (2003) considers how communication can also be used for the purpose of deception. Some of my own work discusses both the coordination and the anti-coordination features of communication; see Ellingsen and Östling (2010, 2018). For a recent discussion of conscious as well as unconscious coordination, see Crawford (2016).

---

[4] Ellingsen (1997b) shows my first steps down this road.

The discussion of mediation goes back to Aumann (1974). See also Chapter 6 of Myerson (1991).

Chwe (2001) is a fascinating book on the many social practices that are used to create common knowledge.

Chapter 10. Authority's Limitations

There is surprisingly little game theoretic analysis of authority; I know only of Mailath, Morris, and Postlewaite (2017) and Basu (2018). A deeper understanding probably requires a formalization of legitimacy along lines explored in the philosophy of law (e.g., Hart, 1961); for a suggestion along these lines, see Greif and Rubin (2022). See also Hadfield and Weingast (2014) and the references therein. Presumably, a satisfactory model needs to consider the role of organized punishment, as discussed in Chapter 12.

As for the point that being able to speak in the future can be bad for commitment today, Andersson and Wengström (2012) is the closest reference that I can think of. The broader point that excessive power is a source of hold-up problems, and thus holds back investment, is the core message of North and Weingast (1989). A version of the basic argument in an institutional context – the optimal location of firm boundaries – was articulated by Grossman and Hart (1986). Williamson (1985, Chapter 6) was earlier in print, but was less fully articulated and possibly benefited from the prior work of Grossman and Hart.

Chapter 11. Relationships

Game theorists early understood that it might be much easier to sustain cooperation in repeated games than in one-shot games. The central publication is Aumann (1959), which formally demonstrated the "Folk theorem": If players are patient, then any payoff vector that is feasible and consistent with individually rational behavior can be sustained as a strong Nash equilibrium of the indefinitely repeated game. Subsequent work introduced impatience ($\delta < 1$) and insisted on subgame-perfect equilibrium (but did not insist on strong equilibrium, i.e., robustness to multi-player deviations), reaching essentially the same conclusion.

A problem in this literature is that almost anything can happen in equilibrium. If we are to make interesting predictions, we must add an analysis of how people coordinate. Experiments involving repeated Prisoners' Dilemmas suggest that strategic risk is an important concern, just as in one-shot Stag Hunt games; see Blonski, Ockenfels, and Spagnolo (2011) and Breitmoser (2015). Such experiments also reveal that people primarily use a few simple strategies, notably "always defect," "tit-for-tat" and "grim" and that miscoordination is a serious concern; see Dal Bó and Fréchette (2019).

A plausible source of strategic risk and miscoordination is that people fail to understand each others' intentions. There is a need for joint clarity. Kreps (1990) is a prescient analysis of corporate culture as a means to generate clarity in ongoing relationships (in fact, the article was written several years earlier). For a recent exposition of this issue, and rich references to the relevant organizational literature, see Gibbons et al. (2021). Presumably, as suggested by Crawford (2016), the literature on coordination in indefinitely repeated games might eventually merge with the literature on coordination in simpler games, described in the notes to Chapter 9.

There are many extensions of the baseline repeated games model, in particular to cases where players cannot observe precisely what others have done (games with imperfect monitoring). In this case it is more difficult to sustain cooperation; for an early analysis and application to cartel stability, see Green and Porter (1984). For surveys of the literature on repeated games, see Fudenberg and Tirole (1991, Chapter 5) and Mailath and Samuelson (2006).

Another extension is to allow the nature of the game to change as a function of the players' past behavior.

For example, in the context of a common-pool resource such as a wood or a lake, past exploitation affects future availability. There is a rich literature on such dynamic resource games. Again, equilibrium selection is a major issue. For example, one might focus on Markov-perfect equilibria, where strategies only depend on the current state rather than the full history; for a characterization, see Dutta and Sundaram (1993). A good port of entry to this literature is Sethi and Somanathan (1996).

A recent literature makes more precise predictions about behavior in realistic relationships by extending the stage-game to admit pre-play communication before players take actions and transfers afterwards; see in particular the work on *contractual equilibrium* by Miller and Watson (2013).

This development was preceded by the literature on relational contracting, which also allowed utility transfers but usually also permitted external enforcement for some of the actions (for example, for promised transfers); see, e.g., MacLeod and Malcomson (1989) and Levin (2003). Watson, Miller, and Olsen (2020) use contractual equilibrium analysis to study the shape of such relational contracts.

Whereas there is a considerable literature on indefinitely repeated games with transfers (see above), theories of the use of costly punishment are rare. The small literature that exists, primarily focuses on specialized enforcers; see next chapter.

There are still many gaps between the theoretical literature and some of the practices that are observed in reality. For example, while Ostrom (1990) observes that well-functioning management of common-pool resources does involve punishment of misbehaving users, first-time violations may merely call for a warning, and only upon repeat offending do punishments get harsh.

As of now, there is also relatively little literature that ties the formal analysis of relationships to cross-cultural comparisons of social regulation. For a discussion of "cultural tightness" in different countries, see Gelfand et al. (2011).

Chapter 12. Third-Party Punishment

This chapter is inspired by Dixit (2003, 2004), who in turn is inspired by Gambetta (1993). A recent related paper is Acemoglu and Wolitzky (2020). The natural monopoly result is original as far as I know (it's been in my lecture notes for two decades, and I ought to have developed it further). The logic is essentially the same as in Klein and Leffler's (1981) analysis of non-contractible quality provision in markets. As they point out, already Adam Smith understood that providers of credence goods must earn a rent in order to remain trustworthy (see the quote in their footnote 3).

Aghion et al. (2010) test several variants of the general hypothesis that people are more likely to want regulation (powerful third parties) when trust is low. They find much support for this idea. In doing so, they cast some doubt on the competing idea that (past) centralization of power is an ultimate cause of current poor performance. It may instead be a symptom of deeper cultural deficiencies. (Of course, it is entirely plausible that causal effects work both ways.)

Avner Greif pioneered the game theoretic analysis of how associations have been able to create collective reputations that facilitate long-distance trade; see Greif (1989, 1993) and Greif, Milgrom, and Weingast (1994). See also Greif (2006a, b).

Chapter 13. Coercion: Costs and Benefits

Excessive taxation, or detrimental coercion more generally, seems under-analyzed in the literature. My example is a trivial application of the Folk theorem, but I imagine that one may make similar progress concerning the use of punishment as Miller and Watson (2013) have made concerning the use of reward.

The analysis of desirable taxation (the failure of the Coase theorem for $n > 2$) follows Ellingsen and Paltseva (2016) – who also offer a detailed survey of the relevant literature – but the particular example with a closed-form solution is new.[5] Many economics textbooks still accept the Coase theorem as being true for all n. Nonetheless, they argue that free-riding prevents voluntary provision of public goods. To reconcile these two positions, they usually appeal to "transaction costs" as being the real culprit that prevents private agreements. I hope that the simple example here can help to convince my colleagues that free-riding is a problem even in a world without transaction costs.

Chapter 14. Contracts and Governance

The chapter provides a glimpse of formal contract theory in relation to the theory of the firm. The basic questions in this literature were originally posed by Coase (1937, 1960). I initially focus on the conversation between Alchian and Demsetz (1972) on one hand and Holmström (1982) on the other.

The objection to Holmström's team incentive scheme reflects a wider concern in the literature on mechanism design that the mechanism ought to have a unique solution. For a survey of the mechanism design literature and its relation to contracts and governance, see Moore (1992).

The combination of relational contracting and asset ownership was first informally discussed by Klein, Crawford, and Alchian (1978). Formal models are due to Halonen (2002) and Baker, Gibbons, and Murphy (2002).[6] The little model of separation between ownership of control is new here as

---

[5] Previous work of mine that was motivated by similar concerns include Ellingsen (1998) and Ellingsen and Paltseva (2012).

[6] A version of Halonen's paper was included already in her doctoral dissertation at LSE from 1993, which reminds me that I shared an office with her until August 1991, when I completed my own dissertation.

far as I know, but there exists a manuscript by Fong, Li, and Schnabl (2008) that touches on similar issues.[7]

The hypothesis that activities will be vertically integrated when assets are costly and relationship-specific is the cornerstone of Williamson's (1971, 1975) (informal) theory of the firm, and it is empirically well supported; see, e.g., Lafontaine and Slade (2007). In a nutshell, Williamson's argument is that negotiations in thin markets tend to be inefficient and that a firm avoids inefficient negotiations through the power of authority that is vested with the firm's owners and their representatives.[8] The little model, in the spirit of Klein, Crawford, and Alchian (1978), fills in some details of that theory: The risk of bargaining breakdown is associated with relatively attractive outside options, while the power of authority stems from the removal of those options.

The role of ownership as a bargaining chip that influences non-contractible investments was first explored by Grossman and Hart (1986) and Hart and Moore (1990). My treatment here builds entirely on Hart, Shleifer, and Vishny (1997).[9] The chapter does not attempt to cover the more "behavioral" models of the firm. For some pointers, see the above notes on the literature to Chapter 8.

Perhaps the greatest omission is that I don't address the "standard" principal agent model, where actions are unverifiable but it is possible to verify outcomes that are imperfectly correlated with actions. The multi-task version of that model,

---

[7] Klein, Crawford, and Alchian's informal analysis goes so far as to discuss the benefits of joint versus separate ownership, but does not observe that outside ownership can be even better.

[8] A decade later, possibly influenced by Grossman and Hart (1986), Williamson also discussed a drawback of integration, namely that authority can be abused.

[9] Maskin and Tirole (1999) have argued that in the context of one-sided unverifiable investment, which affects the gains from trade, the verifiability problem might be circumvented by contracts that only depend on messages that the contracting parties send to the enforcer, relieving courts from verifying any other facts. However, the functioning of these contracts might depend too heavily on the assumption that parties do not care about reciprocity; see Fehr, Powell, and Wilkening (2021).

due to Holmström and Milgrom (1991) is one of my all-time favorite papers.

Chapter 15. Limited Liability and Corporate Finance

The modern corporate finance literature starts with Jensen and Meckling (1976), who argue that financial contracts are designed to mitigate the conflict of interest between investors and managers. However, their analysis rests on several ad hoc assumptions. The literature on optimal security design thus starts with Townsend (1979). For an encyclopaedic textbook treatment of financial contracting models that were developed at rapid pace over the next 25 years, see Tirole (2006).

The ex ante diversion model displayed here is a stripped-down version of Tirole (2001), which in turn builds on several earlier models. I have a particular fondness for the idea that financial contracting is designed to avoid diversion at the investment stage, as this is the premise for my work with Burkart on trade credit; see Burkart and Ellingsen (2004).

The simple ex post diversion model is related to Shleifer and Wolfenzon (2002); see also Ellingsen and Kristiansen (2011).

References to the work mentioned in the Food for Thought include Banerjee, Duflo, and Sharma (2021) and Banerjee and Iyer (2005).

Chapter 16. Asymmetric Information

The literature on asymmetric information is enormous, even when we confine attention to pure screening and signaling problems. Pioneering insights into these trading frictions are Akerlof (1970), Spence (1974), and Rothschild and Stiglitz (1976). Zahavi (1975) originates the study of signaling in biology.

There is a large literature on why and how people signal their charity, either because they want to influence others' behavior – as in our courtship example – or merely want others to think well about them. Landmark contributions include Camerer (1988), Bernheim (1994), Glazer and Konrad (1996), Carmichael and MacLeod (1997), Bénabou and Tirole (2006), and Andreoni and Bernheim (2009). My own work includes Ellingsen and Johannesson (2007, 2008b, 2011).

For a textbook treatment of the screening problem, see Fudenberg and Tirole (1991, Chapter 7). Subsequent chapters of the same book provide an advanced treatment of signaling problems.[10]

Another important problem concerns costless pre-play communication – cheap talk – when parties have different information. This literature started with Crawford and Sobel (1982), who demonstrated how the degree of rational information revelation is connected to the degree of alignment of the parties' interests. Following Kamenica and Gentzkow (2011), there has been much recent interest in the related question of how much information organizations will choose to reveal – for example, how coarsely a school will grade its students or a rating organization will grade the riskiness of borrowers' debt; for a review, see Kamenica (2019).[11]

As noted in the text, distortions due to asymmetric information can be largely overcome if people are honest or otherwise refrain from taking advantage of their private information. Experiments on bilateral bargaining with asymmetric information have documented a remarkable degree of honesty; see Radner and Schotter (1989) and Valley et al. (2002).

---

[10] My modest contribution to this literature is to show that, contrary to conventional wisdom, price may in principle serve as a quality signal even in markets where each customer wants a single unit (Ellingsen, 1997c).

[11] A difference between the initial cheap talk literature and the subsequent "Bayesian persuasion" literature is that the latter assumes that the sender can commit to the coarseness of revelation before learning the actual information.

Gneezy (2005) experimentally studies the aversion to lying when only one party has private information.

In my experimental work, I have studied how honesty depends on the quality of people's relationship (Ellingsen et al., 2009) as well as how people find ways to justify their dishonesty (Lundquist, Ellingsen, and Johannesson, 2009).

Postface

Despite the focus on ideas rather than persons, the text makes references to several Enlightenment philosophers and historical events as well as some of the greatest modern scholars. The names are mostly male, and mostly European and American. If I had instead written a survey of the most exciting recent research, the balance would have been different. One of the field's few female pioneers, Elinor Ostrom (1933–2012), could not even take a doctoral degree in her favorite discipline, economics. Where she came from, girls were blocked from the mathematics courses that the doctoral programs in economics required. By 2009, when she became the first woman to receive the *Sveriges Riksbank Prize in Memory of Alfred Nobel*, the environment had changed. Two years earlier, in 2007, Susan Athey had become the first woman to be awarded the *John Bates Clark Medal* (the most prestigious prize for economists below the age of 40). In 2020, when Melissa Dell received the Clark medal for her groundbreaking work on the long-run economic impact of historical institutions, she became the fifth female recipient. Fortunately, institutions can change.

Acknowledgments

Over the years, I have benefited immensely from working with brilliant colleagues. The collaborators who have most strongly influenced the material in this book are Magnus Johannesson, Eirik Gaard Kristiansen, Topi Miettinen, Erik Mohlin, Elena Paltseva, and Robert Östling. I am also grateful to the many students who have asked difficult questions in my courses Economics of Organization and Theory of Institutions.

As a doctoral student, I wanted to study the theory of the firm. I was influenced by the thinking of my thesis supervisor, John Moore. However, at the time I was unable to work creatively on the topic. Fortunately, my start as an assistant professor teaching organizational economics coincided with the publication of *Economics, Organization, and Management* by Paul Milgrom and John Roberts, an unusual combination of textbook and monograph. The book was revolutionary. By scaling back the math and widening the thematic scope, Milgrom and Roberts provided an account of modern microeconomics that was more compelling to both practitioners and readers outside of economics than any other economics text at the time. The book influenced me immensely, but it retained one peculiarity of economics teaching; it started from the benchmark of perfectly organized markets. If the purpose is to understand why some societies or organizations function better than others, surely that cannot be the right place to start? Even for those who believe that the key to prosperity is to let markets allocate most of the goods, it is essential to understand how one can move from a dysfunctional self-catering society to a well-functioning market economy. I therefore decided to do the opposite, i.e., to start with an analysis of complete anarchy. In other words, I follow the example of the Enlightenment philosophers Hobbes and Locke, rather than that of the great modern economists Samuelson and Arrow.

Over the years, conversations with Ernst Fehr, Oliver Hart, Bengt Holmström, and Klaus Schmidt have helped me to sharpen my arguments at critical junctures.

Borrowing liberally is allowed in textbooks. Still, some debts are too large to be ignored. For this book, my role models are Colin Camerer, Avinash Dixit, and Thomas Schelling. All three use game theory as a lens through which to see the world more clearly. All three strive for the greatest possible simplicity. And all three have been venturing far away from (what was once considered) economics to study problems at the core of the social sciences. Thomas Schelling's book *The Strategy of Conflict* from 1960 seeks to understand war and peace. It remains one of the great classics in social sciences, mysteriously deep and accessible at the same time. Avinash Dixit's book *Lawlessness and Economics* from 2004 uses simple models to confront basic questions concerning the creation of social order, covering several of the same issues that I address here. Finally, Colin Camerer's book from 2003, *Behavioral Game Theory*, organizes the first five decades of experimental evidence on behavior in games and confronts it with the various theories that were available at the time. The need for better formal theories of social behavior has never been explained more clearly.

Some things one should not borrow. I have struggled long and hard to find a suitable title for this book and thought that I had finally succeeded with *Pillars of Prosperity*. I am grateful to Torsten Persson for reminding me that Besley and Persson (2011) beat me by a decade. At least I had already given up on my idea for a book cover. The ideal classical painting, *The Allegory of Good and Bad Government* by Ambrogio Lorenzetti, was used as a book cover two decades ago by Bowles (2004).

I am immensely grateful to the people who have helped me create the book. First and foremost, Avinash Dixit made several superb suggestions, both intellectual and practical on how to write it. Ask Ellingsen, Erik Mohlin, and Robert Östling made exceptionally detailed and insightful comments on early drafts. Once the first draft was done, Jaime Marshall, my theretofore only contact in the world of book publishing, graciously helped me to understand the nature of my book as well as pointing me in the direction of the right publisher. To my surprise, that publisher turned out to be Polity, whose editor Ian Malcolm offered superb advice throughout. Ian also solicited four anonymous yet wonderfully helpful reviewers. Their input and enthusiasm got me across the finishing line. Warm thanks for helpful comments also to Emil Bustos, Johan Callermo, Matthew Jackson, Tove Forsbacka Karlsson, Gustav Karreskog, Elena Paltseva, Lisa Román, Joakim Semb, Daniel Spiro, and Fabian Wiedemeier.

The life of a researcher is only possible if someone is willing to pay for the time we spend thinking. Over the years, I have received generous financial support from the Ragnar Söderberg Foundation and from the Jan Wallander and Tom Hedelius Foundation. For this book, I have also benefited from the support of the Global Challenges Foundation.

Answers to Exercises

Here are the answers to the exercises. If you read a pdf-copy of the book, you may simply click on the Exercise number to get back to where you were.

Possible answers for Exercise 3.1:
1. $U_i = c_i$.
2. $U_i = c_i + \alpha_i \sum_{j \neq i} c_j$, where the sum is over some set of *other* people that i cares about.
3. $U_i = \min\{c_j\}_{j \in N}$, that is, the *lowest* consumption level for any person that i cares about (including herself).

Answer for Exercise 4.1: Matrix 1 is a game (numbers are utilities). Matrix 2 is a situation (numbers are consequences).

Answer for Exercise 4.2: Rational altruist Rowena maximizes her expected utility (4.1). If Colin plays S, it is better for Rowena to play S if $2 + 2\alpha > 3$. If Colin plays N, it is better for Rowena to play S if $3\alpha > 1 + \alpha$. Therefore:

(i) If $\alpha > 1/2$, Rowena plays S regardless of what she believes Colin will do.

(ii) If $\alpha < 1/2$, Rowena plays N regardless of what she believes Colin will do.

Answer for Exercise 4.3: Rational egalitarian Rowena maximizes her expected utility (4.2).

(i) If $\beta < 1/3$, Rowena plays N regardless of what she believes Colin will do.

(ii) If $\beta > 1/3$, Rowena's behavior depends on what she believes Colin will do. In particular, she plays N if she feels certain that Colin plays N, and she plays S if she feels certain that Colin plays S.

Answer for Exercise 4.4: Rational and selfish norm-abider Rowena maximizes her expected utility (4.3).

(i) If $\varphi\mu < 1$, Rowena plays N regardless of what she believes Colin will do.

(ii) If $\varphi\mu > 1$, Rowena plays S regardless of what she believes Colin will do.

Answer for Exercise 4.5: (i) If Rowena and Colin only feel bad about violating the norm if the opponent abides by it, the game is:

	S	N
S	2,2	$0, 3 - \phi\mu$
N	$3 - \phi\mu, 0$	1,1

Figure 20.2 The Conditional norm-abiders' social dilemma game

(iia) If $\varphi\mu < 1$, Rowena plays N regardless of what she believes Colin will do.

(iib) If $\varphi\mu > 1$, Rowena plays S if she believes that Colin will play S with probability at least $1/\varphi\mu$.

Answer for Exercise 6.1: There are two Nash equilibria in pure strategies (H, H) and (L, L).

Answer for Exercise 6.2: There are two Nash equilibria in pure strategies (B, L) and (T, R).

Answer for Exercise 6.3: (i) No player has a dominant strategy. (Dominance requires that the strategy is always better than the other strategies. Colin's strategy NN is *weakly dominant*, since it is never worse than any of the other strategies, and sometimes better.) (ii) Colin's strategy SS is dominated.

Answer for Exercise 6.4: Let Colin's strategies be written on the form ij where i denotes what he does if Rowena plays L and j denotes what he does if Rowena plays R. (i) The strategy profile (L, LR) is a subgame-perfect equilibrium. (ii) The strategy profile (R, RR) is a Nash equilibrium that is not subgame-perfect. (Colin would not find it optimal to play R if Rowena deviated to play L. The unique subgame-perfect equilibrium *outcome* is (L, L).

Answer for Exercise 7.1: (i) 2. (ii) 1.2. (iii) $\{(u_1, u_2)|0 \leq u_1 + u_2 \leq 2\}$; this is the feasible set of utilities in Figure 7.1.

Answer for Exercise 10.1: (i) If Colin has absolute authority, you might think that Colin will get $3 + 3 = 6$, but that is a mistake. Ask yourself: Why would Rowena ever play S if she thinks that she obtains no reward in Stage 2? Clearly, she will rather play N at Stage 1. But you are right to think that Colin will communicate (T, R) for Stage 2. Thus, Colin obtains a payoff of $0 + 3 = 3$ and Rowena obtains $1 + 1 = 2$. (ii) Colin gets $0 + 1 = 1$ and Rowena gets $1 + 3 = 4$.

Answer for Exercise 11.1: (i) Start at the end. Colin prefers to play NR no matter what Rowena has done. Since Rowena understands that Colin will play NR no matter what, her best strategy is to play NS. Thus, the unique subgame-perfect equilibrium is (NS, NR). (ii) Now, make the same argument, starting at Stage 2 in Period 10. See how backward induction implies that (*NS*, *NR*) is played every period. Thus, there is only one subgame-perfect equilibrium.

Answer for Exercise 11.2: The answer is analogous to the answer to Exercise 11.1(i).

Answer for Exercise 14.1: The profit function is

$$p = a_R + a_C - \frac{1}{2}a_R^2 - \frac{1}{2}a_C^2.$$

(i) The first-order condition with respect to a_R is

$$1 - a_R = 0.$$

The second-order condition is fulfilled. Thus, $a_R^* = 1$. The same analysis for a_C yields $a_C^* = 1$.

(ii) Rowena's problem is to maximize

$$\alpha p = \alpha\left(a_R + a_C - \frac{1}{2}a_R^2 - \frac{1}{2}a_C^2\right).$$

Clearly, the first- and second-order conditions are exactly the same as for the profit-maximization problem. The same logic holds for Colin. Thus the strategy profile (a_R^*, a_R^*) also constitutes an equilibrium in dominant strategies.

Answer for Exercise 16.1: What is the maximal level of education that a low-productivity worker would take in order to get a wage of 2 instead of 1? Since the cost of education is e/p and $p = 1$, the equation is $2 - e = 1$. Thus, the answer is that the high-productivity worker takes an education $e = 1$ and the low-productivity worker takes no education $e = 0$.

References

Abeler, J., Nosenzo, D., and Raymond, C. (2019). Preferences for Truth-Telling, *Econometrica* 87, 1115–1153.

Acemoglu, D., Johnson, S., and Robinson, J.A. (2001). The Colonial Origins of Comparative Development: An Empirical Investigation, *American Economic Review* 91, 1369–1401.

Acemoglu, D. Gallego, F.A., and Robinson, J.A. (2014). Institutions, Human Capital, and Development, *Annual Reviews of Economics* 6, 875–912.

Acemoglu, D. and Robinson, J.A. (2012). *Why Nations Fail: The Origins of Power, Prosperity, and Poverty*, New York: Crown Publishing.

Acemoglu, D. and Wolitzsky, A. (2020). Sustaining Cooperation: Community Enforcement versus Specialized Enforcement, *Journal of the European Economic Association* 18, 1078–1122.

Adams, J.S. (1963). Wage Inequities, Productivity and Work Quality, *Industrial Relations* 3, 9–16.

Adams, J.S. and Rosenbaum, W.E. (1962). The Relationship of Worker Productivity to Cognitive Dissonance about Wage Inequities, *Journal of Applied Psychology* 46, 161–164.

Aghion, P., Algan, Y., Cahuc, P., and Shleifer, A. (2010). Regulation and Distrust, *Quarterly Journal of Economics* 125, 1015–1049.

Alchian, A.A. and Demsetz, H. (1972). Production, Information Costs, and Economic Organization, *American Economic Review* 62, 777–795.

Alesina, A. and Giuliano, P. (2015). Culture and Institutions, *Journal of Economic Literature* 53, 898–944.

Alger, I. and Weibull, J.W. (2013). Homo Moralis – Preference Evolution Under Incomplete Information and Assortative Matching, *Econometrica* 81, 2269–2302.

Akerlof, G.A. (1970). The Market for "Lemons": Quality Uncertainty and the Market Mechanism, *Quarterly Journal of Economics* 89, 488–500.

Akerlof, G.A. (1982). Labor Contracts as Partial Gift Exchange, *Quarterly Journal of Economics* 97, 543–569.

Akerlof, G. and Kranton, R. (2000). Economics and Identity, *Quarterly Journal of Economics* 115(3), 715–753.

Andersson, O. and Wengström, E. (2012). Credible Communication and Cooperation: Experimental Evidence from Multi-stage Games, *Journal of Economic Behavior and Organization* 81, 207–219.

Andreoni, J. and Bernheim, B.D. (2009). Social Image and the 50–50 Norm: A Theoretical and Experimental Analysis of Audience Effects, *Econometrica* 77, 1607–1636.

Andreoni, J., Rao, J.M., and Trachtman, H. (2017). Avoiding the Ask: A Field Experiment on Altruism, Empathy, and Charitable Giving, *Journal of Political Economy* 125, 625–653.

Aumann, R.J. (1959). Acceptable Points in General Cooperative *n*-Person Games, in H.W. Kuhn and R.D. Luce (eds.), *Contributions to the Theory of Games IV* 287–324, Princeton: Princeton University Press.

Aumann, R.J. (1974). Subjectivity and Correlation in Randomized Strategies, *Journal of Mathematical Economics* 1, 67–96.

Babcock, L. and Loewenstein, G. (1997). Explaining Bargaining Impasse: The Role of Self-Serving Biases, *Journal of Economic Perspectives* 11, 109–26.

Babcock, L., Loewenstein, G., Issacharoff, S., and Camerer, C. (1995). Biased Judgments of Fairness in Bargaining, *American Economic Review* 85, 1337–43.

Bacon, F. (1620). *Instauratio Magna: Novum Organum Sive Indicia Vera de Interpretatione Naturae*, London: John Bill. A modern English edition is L. Jardine and M. Silverthorne (eds.), *The New Organon*, Cambridge: Cambridge University Press, 2000.

Bahrami-Rad, D., Beauchamp, J., Henrich, J., and Schulz, J. (2022). Kin-based Institutions and Economic Development, https://ssrn.com/abstract=4200629.

Baker, G., Gibbons, R., and Murphy, K.J. (2002). Relational Contracts and the Theory of the Firm, *Quarterly Journal of Economics* 117, 39–84.

Bandiera, O., Mohnen, M., Rasul, I., and Viarengo, M. (2019). Nation-Building Through Compulsory Schooling During the Age of Mass Migration, *Economic Journal* 129, 62–109.

Banerjee, A., Duflo, E., and Sharma, G. (2021). Long-Term Effects of the Targeting the Ultra Poor Program, *American Economic Review: Insights* 3, 471–486.

Banerjee, A. and Iyer, L. (2005). History, Institutions, and Economic Performance: The Legacy of Colonial Land Tenure Systems in India, *American Economic Review* 95, 1190–1213.

Banfield, E.C. (1958). *The Moral Basis of a Backward Society*, Glencoe IL: Free Press.

Basu, K. (2018). *The Republic of Beliefs: A New Approach to Law and Economics*, Princeton University Press, Princeton.

Basu, S. et al. (2009). Recordkeeping Alters Economic History by Promoting Reciprocity, *PNAS* 106, 1009–1014.

Bénabou, R. and Tirole, J. (2006). Incentives and Prosocial Behavior, *American Economic Review* 96, 1652–1678.

Bénabou, R. and Tirole, J. (2016). Mindful Economics: The Production, Consumption, and Value of Beliefs, *Journal of Economic Perspectives* 30, 141–164.

Berg, J.E., Dickhaut, J., and McCabe, K. (1995). Trust, Reciprocity, and Social History, *Games and Economic Behavior* 10, 122–142.

Bernheim, B.D. (1994). A Theory of Conformity, *Journal of Political Economy* 102, 841–877.

Besley, T. and Persson, T. (2011). *Pillars of Prosperity: The Political Economics of Development Clusters*, Princeton NJ: Princeton University Press.

Bicchieri, C. (2005). *The Grammar of Society: The Nature and Dynamics of Social Norms*, Cambridge MA: Cambridge University Press.

Bisin, A. and Verdier, T. (2001). The Economics of Cultural Transmission and the Dynamics of Preferences, *Journal of Economic Theory* 97, 298–319.

Blattman, C. and Miguel, E. (2010). Civil War, *Journal of Economic Literature* 48, 3–57.

Blonski, M., Ockenfels, P., and Spagnolo, G. (2011). Equilibrium Selection in the Repeated Prisoner's Dilemma: Axiomatic Approach and Experimental Evidence, *American Economic Journal: Microeconomics* 3, 164–92.

Bloom, N. and van Reenen, J. (2010). Why Do Management Practices Differ Across Firms and Countries? *Journal of Economic Perspectives* 24 (Winter), 203–224.

Bolton, G.E. and Ockenfels, A. (2000). ERC: A Theory of Equity, Reciprocity, and Competition, *American Economic Review* 90: 166–193.

Bowles, S. (2004). *Microeconomics: Behavior, Institutions and Evolution*, Princeton NJ: Princeton University Press.

Breitmoser, Y. (2015). Cooperation, But No Reciprocity: Individual Strategies in the Repeated Prisoner's Dilemma, *American Economic Review* 105, 2882–2910.

Brekke, K.A., Kverndokk, S., and Nyborg, K. (2003). An Economic Model of Moral Motivation, *Journal of Public Economics* 9–10, 1967–1983.

Broberg, T., Ellingsen, T., and Johannesson, M. (2007). Is Generosity Involuntary? *Economics Letters* 94, 32–37.

Burkart, M. and Ellingsen, T. (2004). In-Kind Finance: A Theory of Trade Credit, *American Economic Review* 94, 569–590.

Camerer, C.F. (1988). Gifts as Economic Signals and Social Symbols, *American Journal of Sociology* 94 (Supplement), S180–S214.

Camerer, C.F. (2003). *Behavioral Game Theory*, Princeton: Princeton University Press.

Carmichael, H.L. and MacLeod, W.B. (1997). Gift Giving and the Evolution of Cooperation, *International Economic Review* 38, 485–509.

Cason, T., Sharma, T., and Vadovic, R. (2020). Correlated Beliefs: Predicting Outcomes in 2×2 Games, *Games and Economic Behavior* 122, 256–276.

Chaudhuri, A. (2011). Sustaining Cooperation in Laboratory Public Goods Experiments: A Selective Survey of the Literature, *Experimental Economics* 14, 47–83.

Charness, G. and Rabin, M. (2002). Understanding Social Preferences with Simple Tests, *Quarterly Journal of Economics* 117, 817–869.

Chwe, M.S. (2001). *Rational Ritual: Culture, Coordination and Common Knowledge*, Princeton: Princeton University Press.

Cicero, M. Tullius (44 BCE/1913). *On Duty*. English Translation: Walter Miller, Cambridge MA: Harvard University Press.

Coase, R. (1937). The Nature of the Firm, *Economica* 4, 386–405.

Coase, R. (1960). The Problem of Social Cost, *Journal of Law and Economics* 3, 1–44.

Cohn, A., Maréchal, M.A., Tannenbaum, D., and Zünd, C.L. (2019). Civic Honesty around the Globe, *Science* 365 (6448), 70–73.

Coleman, J.S. (1988). Social Capital in the Creation of Human Capital, *American Journal of Sociology* 94 (Supplement), S95–S120.

Cox, J.C., Friedman, D., and Gjerstad, S. (2007). A Tractable Model of Reciprocity and Fairness, *Games and Economic Behavior* 59, 17–45.

Cox, J.C., Kerschbamer, R., and Neururer, D. (2016). What Is Trustworthiness and What Drives It? *Games and Economic Behavior* 98, 197–218.

Crawford, V.P. (1982). A Theory of Disagreement in Bargaining, *Econometrica* 50, 607–637.

Crawford, V.P. (2003). Lying for Strategic Advantage: Rational and Boundedly Rational Misrepresentation of Intentions, *American Economic Review* 93, 133–149.

Crawford, V.P. (2016). New Directions for Modelling Strategic Behavior: Game-Theoretic Models of Communication, Coordination, and Cooperation in Economic Relationships, *Journal of Economic Perspectives* 30, 131–150.

Crawford, V.P. and Sobel, J. (1982). Strategic Information Transmission, *Econometrica* 50, 1431–1451.

Cyert, R.M. and March, J.G. (1963). *A Behavioral Theory of the Firm*, Englewood Cliffs, NJ: Prentice-Hall.

Dal Bó, P. and Fréchette, G. (2019). Strategy Choice in the Infinitely Repeated Prisoner's Dilemma, *American Economic Review* 109, 3929–3952.

Dana, J., Cain, D.M., and Dawes, R.M. (2006). What You Don't Know Won't Hurt Me: Costly (but Quiet) Exit in Dictator Games, *Organizational Behavior and Human Decision Processes* 100, 193–201.

Dana, J., Weber, R.A., and Kuang, J.X. (2007). Exploiting Moral Wiggle Room: Experiments Demonstrating an Illusory Preference for Fairness, *Economic Theory* 33, 67–80.

Darwin, C.R. (1871). *The Descent of Man, and Selection in Relation to Sex*, London: John Murray.

Deb, J. and Basak, D. (2020). Gambling over Public Opinion, *American Economic Review* 110, 3492–3521.

Dell, M. and Querubin, P. (2018). Nation Building Through Foreign Intervention: Evidence from Discontinuities in Military Strategies, *Quarterly Journal of Economics* 133, 701–764.

DellaVigna, S., List, J.A., and Malmendier, U. (2012). Testing for Altruism and Social Pressure in Charitable Giving, *Quarterly Journal of Economics* 127, 1–56.

Deutsch, M. (1958). Trust and Suspicion, *Journal of Conflict Resolution* 2, 265–279.

Dijk, E. van and de Dreu, C.K.W. (2021). Experimental Games and Social Psychology, *Annual Review of Psychology* 72, 415–438.

Dixit, A.K. (2003). On Modes of Economic Governance, *Econometrica* 71, 449–471.

Dixit, A.K. (2004). *Lawlessness and Economics: Alternative Modes of Governance*, Princeton: Princeton University Press.

Dixit, A.K. and Nalebuff, B.J. (2010). *The Art of Strategy: A Game Theorist's Guide to Success in Business and Life*, New York: W.W. Norton.

Dixit, A.K., Skeath, S., and Reiley Jr., J. (2021). *Games of Strategy*, Fourth Edition, New York: W.W. Norton.

Dreber, A., Ellingsen, T., Johannesson, M., and Rand, D.G. (2013). Do People Care about Social Context? Framing Effects in Dictator Games, *Experimental Economics* 16, 349–371.

Durkheim, E. (1900/1958). *Professional Ethics and Civil Morals*, Glencoe IL: Free Press. (Note: The manuscript was completed around 1900, but was first published in French in 1950.)

Durkheim, E. (1893/1960). *The Division of Labor in Society*, Glencoe IL: The Free Press.

Durlauf, S. and Fafchamps, M. (2005). Social Capital, in *Handbook of Economic Growth*, P. Aghion and S. Durlauf (eds.), 639–699.

Dutta, P.K. and Sundaram, R.K. (1993). A Tragedy of the Commons? *Economic Theory* 3, 413–426.

Ellingsen, T. (1991). Strategic Buyers and the Social Cost of Monopoly, *American Economic Review* 81, 648–657.

Ellingsen, T. (1994). Cardinal Utility: A History of Hedonimetry, in M. Allais and O. Hagen (eds.), *Cardinalism: A Fundamental Approach*, 105–165, Dordrecht: Kluwer.

Ellingsen, T. (1997a). Efficiency Wages and X-Inefficiencies, *Scandinavian Journal of Economics* 99, 581–596.

Ellingsen, T. (1997b). The Evolution of Bargaining Behavior, *Quarterly Journal of Economics* 112, 581–602.

Ellingsen, T. (1997c). Price Signals Quality: The Case of Perfectly Inelastic Demand, *International Journal of Industrial Organization* 16, 43–61.

Ellingsen, T. (1998). Externalities vs Internalities: A Theory of Political Integration, *Journal of Public Economics* 68, 251–268, 1998.

Ellingsen, T. and Johannesson, M. (2004a). Is There a Hold-up

Problem? *Scandinavian Journal of Economics* 106, 475–494, 2004.

Ellingsen, T. and Johannesson, M. (2004b). Promises, Threats and Fairness, *Economic Journal* 114, 397–420, 2004.

Ellingsen, T. and Johannesson, M. (2005). Does Impartial Deliberation Breed Fair Behavior? An Experimental Test, *Rationality and Society* 17, 116–136.

Ellingsen, T. and Johannesson, M. (2007). Paying Respect, *Journal of Economic Perspectives* 21, 135–149, 2007.

Ellingsen, T. and Johannesson, M. (2008a). Verbal Feedback Induces Prosocial Behavior, *Evolution and Human Behavior* 29, 100–105.

Ellingsen, T. and Johannesson, M. (2008b). Pride and Prejudice: The Human Side of Incentive Theory. *American Economic Review* 98, 990–1008.

Ellingsen, T. and Johannesson, M. (2011). Conspicuous Generosity, *Journal of Public Economics* 95, 1131–1143.

Ellingsen, T., Johannesson, M., Mollerstrom, J., and Munkhammar, S. (2012). Social Framing Effects: Preferences or Beliefs? *Games and Economic Behavior* 76, 117–130.

Ellingsen, T., Johannesson, M., Mollerstrom, J., and Munkhammar, S. (2013). Gender Differences in Social Framing Effects, *Economics Letters* 118, 470–472.

Ellingsen, T. and Kristiansen, E.G. (2022). Fair and Square: A Retention Model of Managerial Compensation, *Management Science* 68, 3604–3624.

Ellingsen, T. and Miettinen, T. (2008). Commitment and Conflict in Bilateral Bargaining, *American Economic Review* 98, 1629–1635.

Ellingsen, T. and Miettinen, T. (2014). Tough Negotiations: Bilateral Bargaining with Durable Commitments, *Games and Economic Behavior* 87, 353–366.

Ellingsen, T. and Mohlin, E. (2022). A Model of Social Duties, manuscript, Stockholm School of Economics.

Ellingsen, T. and Östling, R. (2010). When Does Communication Improve Coordination?, *American Economic Review* 100, 1695–1724.

Ellingsen, T. and Östling, R. (2011). Strategic Risk and Coordination Failure in Blame Games, *Economic Letters* 110, 90–92.

Ellingsen, T., Östling, R., and Wengström, E. (2018). How Does Communication Affect Beliefs in One-Shot Games with Complete Information? *Games and Economic Behavior* 107, 153–181.

Ellingsen, T. and Paltseva, E. (2016). Confining the Coase Theorem: Contracting, Ownership, and Free-riding, *Review of Economic Studies* 83, 547–586.

Ellingsen, T. and Robles, J. (2002). Does Evolution Solve the Hold-up Problem? *Games and Economic Behavior* 39, 28–53, 2002.

Elster, J. (1989). *The Cement of Society*, Cambridge: Cambridge University Press.

Engel, C. (2011). Dictator Games: A Meta Study, *Experimental Economics* 14, 583–610.

Enke, B. (2019). Kinship, Cooperation, and the Evolution of Moral Systems, *Quarterly Journal of Economics* 134, 953–1019.

Falk, A., Fehr, E., and Fischbacher, U. (2003). On the Nature of Fair Behavior, *Economic Inquiry* 41, 20–26.

Falk, A., Fehr, E., and Fischbacher, U. (2008). Testing Theories of Fairness: Intentions Matter, *Games and Economic Behavior* 62, 287–303.

Falk, A. et al. (2018). Global Evidence on Economic Preferences, *Quarterly Journal of Economics* 133, 1645–1692.

Farr, J. (2004). Social Capital: A Conceptual History, *Political Theory* 32, 6–33.

Farrell, J. (1988). Communication, Coordination and Nash Equilibrium, *Economic Letters* 27, 209–214.

Fehr, E. (2018). Behavioral Foundations of Corporate Culture, UBS Center Public Paper no 7, University of Zurich.

Fehr, E., Kirchsteiger, G., and Riedl, A. (1993). Does Fairness Prevent Market Clearing? An Experimental Investigation, *Quarterly Journal of Economics* 108, 437–459.

Fehr, E., Powell, M., and Wilkening, T. (2021). Behavioral Constraints on the Design of Subgame-Perfect Implementation Mechanisms, *American Economic Review* 111, 1055–1091.

Fehr, E. and Schmidt, K.M. (1999). A Theory of Fairness, Competition and Cooperation, *The Quarterly Journal of Economics* 114, 817–868.

Fischbacher, U. and Föllmi-Heusi, F. (2013). Lies in Disguise – An Experimental Study on Cheating, *Journal of the European Economic Association* 11, 525–547.

Fong, Y., Li, J., and Schnabl, P.A. (2008). Relational Contracts and Replaceability, manuscript, Northwestern University.

Frank, R.H. (1988). *Passions within Reason: The Strategic Role of the Emotions*, New York: W.W. Norton.

Friebel, G., Heinz, M., Krüger, M., and Zubanov, N. (2017). Team Incentives and Performance: Evidence from a Retail Chain, *American Economic Review* 107, 2168–2203.

Fudenberg, D. and Tirole, J. (1991), *Game Theory*. Cambridge MA: MIT Press.

Frydlinger, D. and Hart, O. (2023). Overcoming Contractual Incompleteness: The Role of Guiding Principles, *Journal of Law, Economics and Organization* forthcoming.

Gächter, S. and Schulz, J.F. (2016). Intrinsic Honesty and the Prevalence of Rule Violations across Societies, *Nature* 531(7595), 496–499.

Gambetta, D. (ed.) (1988a). *Trust: Making and Breaking Cooperative Relations*, Oxford: Basil Blackwell.

Gambetta, D. (ed.) (1988b). Mafia: The Price of Distrust, Chapter 10 in Gambetta (1988a), pp. 158–175.

Gambetta, D. (1993). *The Sicilian Mafia: The Business of Private Protection*, Cambridge MA: Harvard University Press.

Garfinkel, M.R. and Skaperdas, S. (2007). Economics of Conflict: An Overview, in T. Sandler and K. Hartley (eds.), *Handbook of Defense Economics* vol. II, 649–709.

Gelfand, M.J. et al. (2011). Differences between Tight and Loose Cultures: A 33-Nation Study, *Science* 332(6033), 1100–1104.

Gibbons, R., Grieder, M., Herz, H., and Zehnder, C. (2021). Building an Equilibrium: Rules versus Principles in Relational Contracts, *Organization Science* (Articles in Advance, https://doi.org/10.1287/orsc.2021.1503).

Glazer, A. and Konrad, K.A. (1996). A Signaling Explanation for Charity, *American Economic Review* 86, 1019–1028.

Gneezy, A., Gneezy, U., Riener, G., and Nelson, L.D. (2012). Pay-What-You-Want, Identity, and Self-Signaling in Markets, *Proceedings of the National Academy of Sciences* 109, 7236–7240.

Gneezy, U. (2005). Deception: The Role of Consequences, *American Economic Review* 95, 384–394.

Golman, R., Hagmann, D., and Loewenstein, G. (2017). Information Avoidance, *Journal of Economic Literature* 55, 96–135.

Grech, P.D. and Nax, H.H. (2020). Rational Altruism? On Preference Estimation and Dictator Game Experiments, *Games and Economic Behavior* 119, 309–338.

Green, E. and Porter, R. (1984). Noncooperative Collusion under Imperfect Price Information, *Econometrica* 52, 87–100.

Greif, A. (1993). Contract Enforceability and Economic Institutions in Early Trade: The Maghribi Traders' Coalition, *American Economic Review* 83, 525–548.

Greif, A. (1994). Cultural Beliefs and the Organization of Society: A Historical and Theoretical Reflection on Collectivist and Individualist Societies, *Journal of Political Economy* 102, 912–950.

Greif, A. (2006a). *Institutions and the Path to the Modern Economy: Lessons from Medieval Trade*, Cambridge: Cambridge University Press.

Greif, A. (2006b). The Birth of Impersonal Exchange: The Community Responsibility System and Impartial Justice, *Journal of Economic Perspectives* 20, 221–236.

Greif, A., Milgrom, P., and Weingast, B. (1994). Coordination, Commitment, and Enforcement: The Case of the Merchant Guild, *Journal of Political Economy* 102, 745–776.

Greif, A. and Rubin, J. (2022). Political Legitimacy in Historical Political Economy, forthcoming in *The Oxford Handbook of Historical Political Economy*.

Greif, A. and Tabellini, G. (2010) Cultural and Institutional Bifurcation: China and Europe Compared, *American Economic Review Papers and Proceedings* 100, 135–140.

Grosjean, P. (2014). A History of Violence: The Culture of Honor and Homicide in the South, *Journal of the European Economic Association* 12, 1285–1316.

Grossman, S. and Hart, O. (1986). The Costs and Benefits of Ownership: A Theory of Vertical and Lateral Integration, *Journal of Political Economy* 94, 691–719.

Güth, W., Schmittberger, R., and Schwarze, B. (1982). An Experimental Analysis of Ultimatum Bargaining, *Journal of Economic Behavior and Organization* 3, 367–388.

Haavelmo, T. (1954). *A Study in the Theory of Economic Evolution*, Amsterdam: North-Holland.

Hadfield, G. and Weingast, B. (2014). Microfoundations of the Rule of Law, *Annual Review of Political Science* 17, 21–42.

Hall, R.E. and Jones, C.I. (1999). Why Do Some Countries Produce So Much More Output per Worker than Others? *Quarterly Journal of Economics* 114, 83–116.

Halonen, M. (2002). Reputation and the Allocation of Ownership, *Economic Journal* 112, 539–558.

Harrison, L.E. and Huntington, S.P. (eds.) (2000). *Culture Matters: How Values Shape Human Progress*, New York: Basic Books.

Hart, H.L.A. (1961). *The Concept of Law*, Oxford: Clarendon Press.

Hart, O. and Holmström, B. (2010). A Theory of Firm Scope, *Quarterly Journal of Economics* 125, 483–513.

Hart, O. and Moore, J. (1990). Property Rights and the Theory of the Firm, *Journal of Political Economy* 98, 1119–1158.

Hart, O. and Moore, J. (2008). Contracts as Reference Points, *Quarterly Journal of Economics* 123, 1–48.

Hart, O., Shleifer, A., and Vishny, R.W. (1997). The Proper Scope of Government: Theory and an Application to Prisons, *Quarterly Journal of Economics* 112, 1127–1161.

Henrich, J. (2020). *The WEIRDest People in the World: How the West Became Psychologically Peculiar and Particularly Prosperous*, New York, NY: Farrar, Straus and Giroux.

Hobbes, T. (1651) *Leviathan*, London: Andrew Crooke.

Hofstede, G. (1980). *Culture's Consequences: International Differences in Work-Related Values*, Beverly Hills, CA: Sage Publications (2nd edition 2001).

Holmström, B. (1982). Moral Hazard in Teams, *Bell Journal of Economics* 13, 324–340.

Holmström, B. and Milgrom, P. (1991), Multitask Principal-agent Analyses: Incentive Contracts, Asset ownership, and Job Design, *Journal of Law, Economics, and Organization* (Supplement) 7S, 24–52.

Hume, D. (1740). *A Treatise of Human Nature*, London: Thomas Longman.

Hume, D. (1751). *An Enquiry Concerning the Principles of Morals*, London: A Millar.

Inglehart, R. (2018). *Cultural Evolution: People's Motivations are Changing, and Reshaping the World*, Oxford: Oxford University Press.

Jensen, M.C. and Meckling, W.H. (1976). Theory of the Firm: Managerial Behavior, Agency Costs and Ownership Structure, *Journal of Financial Economics* 3, 305–360.

Joskow, P. (1985). Vertical Integration and Long-term Contracts: The Case of Coal-burning Electric Generating Plants, *Journal of Law, Economics and Organization* 1, 33–80.

Joskow, P. (1987). Contract Duration and Relationship-Specific Investments: Empirical Evidence from Coal Markets, *American Economic Review* 77, 168–185.

Kahneman, D., Knetsch, J.L., and Thaler, R. (1996). Fairness and the Assumptions of Economics, *Journal of Business* 59 (Supplement), S285–S300.

Kamenica, E. (2019). Bayesian Persuasion and Information Design, *Annual Review of Economics* 11, 249–272.

Kamenica, E. and Gentzkow, M. (2011). Bayesian Persuasion, *American Economic Review* 101, 2590–2615.

Kandori, M., Mailath, G., and Rob, R. (1993). Learning, Mutation, and Long-run Equilibria in Games, *Econometrica* 61, 29–56.

Kirchsteiger, G. (1994). The Role of Envy in Ultimatum Games, *Journal of Economic Behavior and Organization* 25, 373–389.

Klein, B., Crawford, R.G., and Alchian, A.A. (1978). Vertical Integration, Appropriable Rents, and the Competitive Contracting Process, *Journal of Law and Economics* 21, 297–326.

Klein, B. and Leffler, K.B. (1981). The Role of Market Forces in Assuring Contractual Performance, *Journal of Political Economy* 89, 615–641.

Knack, S. and Keefer, P. (1997). Does Social Capital Have an Economic Payoff? A Cross-Country Investigation, *Quarterly Journal of Economics* 112, 1251–1288.

Knutsson, D. and Tyrefors, B. (2022). The Quality and Efficiency of Public and Private Firms: Evidence from Ambulance Services, *Quarterly Journal of Economics* 137, 2213–2262.

Kreps, D. (1990). Corporate Culture and Economic Theory, in J. Alt and K. Shepsle (eds.), *Perspectives on Positive Political Economy*, Cambridge: Cambridge University Press.

Krupka, E.L. and Weber, R.A. (2013). Identifying Social Norms Using Coordination Games: Why Does Dictator Game Sharing Vary? *Journal of European Economic Association* 11, 495–524.

Krupka, E.L., Leider, S., and Jiang, M. (2016). A Meeting of the Minds: Informal Agreements and Social Norms, *Management Science* 63, 1708–1729.

La Porta, R., Lopez-de-Silanes, F., Shleifer, A., and Vishny, R. (1999). The Quality of Government, Journal of Law, Economics, and Organization 15, 222–279.

Lafontaine, F. and Slade, M. (2007). Vertical Integration and Firm Boundaries: The Evidence, *Journal of Economic Literature* 45, 629–685.

Landes, D. (2000). Culture Makes Almost All the Difference, Chapter 1 in Harrison and Huntington (2000).

Levin, J. (2003). Relational Incentive Contracts, *American Economic Review* 93, 835–857.

Lewis, W.A. (1955). *The Theory of Economic Growth*, Homewood IL: Richard D. Irwin.

Libecap, G.D. and Wiggins, S.N. (1984). Contractual Responses to the Common Pool: Prorationing of Crude Oil Production, *American Economic Review* 74, 87–98.

Libecap, G.D. and Wiggins, S.N. (1985). The Influence of Private Contractual Failure on Regulation: The Case of Oil Field Unitization, *Journal of Political Economy* 93, 690–714.

Loomis, J.L. (1959). Communication, the Development of Trust, and Co-operative Behavior, *Human Relations* 12, 305–315.

López-Pérez, R. (2008). Aversion to Norm-breaking: A Model, *Games and Economic Behavior* 64, 237–267.

Macaulay, S. (1963). Non-Contractual Relations in Business: A Preliminary Study, *American Sociological Review* 28, 55–67.

MacLeod, W.B. and Malcomson, J.M. (1989). Implicit Contracts, Incentive Compatibility, and Involuntary Unemployment, *Econometrica* 57, 447–80.

Macneil, I.R. (1983). Values in Contract: Internal and External, Northwestern University Law Review 78, 340–418.

Mailath, G.J., Morris, S., and Postlewaite, A. (2017). Laws and Authority, *Research in Economics* 71, 32–42.

Mailath, G.J. and Samuelson, L. (2006). *Repeated Games and Reputations: Long-run Relationships*, Oxford: Oxford University Press.

Malmendier, U. and Schmidt, K.M. (2017). You Owe Me. *American Economic Review* 107, 493–526.

March, J. (1994). *A Primer on Decision-Making: How Decisions Happen*, New York: Free Press.

March, J. and Olsen, J.P. (1989). *Rediscovering Institutions*, New York: Free Press.

Maskin, E. and Tirole, J. (1999). Unforeseen Contingencies and Incomplete Contracts, *Review of Economic Studies* 66, 83–114.

Mauro, P. (1995). Corruption and Growth, *Quarterly Journal of Economics* 110, 681–712.

Mill, J.S. (1848). *Principles of Political Economy*, London: John W. Parker.

Miller, D.A. and Watson, J. (2013). A Theory of Disagreement in Repeated Games with Bargaining, *Econometrica* 81, 2303–2350.

Mokyr, J. (2013). Cultural Entrepreneurs and the Origins of Modern Economic Growth, *Scandinavian Economic History Review* 61, 1–33.

Mokyr, J. (2016). *A Culture of Growth: Origins of the Modern Economy*, Princeton: Princeton University Press.

Moore, J. (1992). Implementation, Contracts, and Renegotiation in Environments with Complete Information, in J.J. Laffont (ed.) *Advances in Economic Theory, Sixth World Congress* volume 1, Econometric Society Monographs.

Murdock, G.P. (1967) Ethnographic Atlas: A Summary, *Ethnology* 6(2), 109–236.

Myerson, R. (1991). *Game Theory: Analysis of Conflict*, Cambridge: Harvard University Press.

Nagel, R., Büren, C., and Frank, B. (2017). Inspired and Inspiring: Hervé Moulin and the Discovery of the Beauty Contest Game, *Mathematical Social Sciences* 90, 191–207.

Nash, J.F. (1950). Equilibrium Points in n-person Games, *PNAS* 36, 48–49.

Nash, J.F. (1953). Two-Person Cooperative Games, *Econometrica* 21, 128–40.

Neumann, J. von and Morgenstern, O. (1947). *Theory of Games and Economic Behavior*, 2nd ed., Princeton: Princeton University Press.

Nietzsche, F. (1887/2003). *On the Genealogy of Morals: A Polemic*, translated from German by H.B. Samuel, New York: Courier Dover Publications.

Nisbet, R.A. (1993). *The Sociological Tradition*, New York: Routledge.

Nöldeke, G. and K. Schmidt (1994). Option Contracts and Renegotiation: A Solution to the Hold-up Problem, *Rand Journal of Economics* 26, 163–172.

North, D.C. (1991). Institutions, *Journal of Economic Perspectives* 5, 97–112.

North, D.C. and Weingast, B.R. (1989). Constitutions and Commitment: The Evolution of Institutions Governing Public Choice in Seventeenth-Century England, *Journal of Economic History* 49, 803–832.

Nunn, N. (2022). On the Dynamics of Human Behavior: The Past, Present, and Future of Culture, Conflict, and Cooperation, *American Economic Association Papers and Proceedings* 112, 15–37.

Nyberg, A.J., Maltarich, M.A., Abdulsalam, D., Essman, S.M., and Cragun, O. (2018). Collective Pay for Performance: A Cross-Disciplinary Review and Meta-Analysis, *Journal of Management* 44, 2433–2472.

Ogilvie, S. and Carus, A.W. (2014). Institutions and Economic Growth in Historical Perspective, Chapter 8 in P. Aghion and S.N. Durlauf (eds.), *Handbook of Economic Growth*, Amsterdam: Elsevier.

Olson, M. (1993). Dictatorship, Democracy, and Development, *American Political Science Review* 87, 567–576.

Osborne, M. and Rubinstein, A. (1994). *A Course in Game Theory*, Cambridge MA: MIT Press.

Ostrom, E. (1990). *Governing the Commons: The Evolution of Institutions for Collective Action*, Cambridge: Cambridge University Press.

Ostrom, E. (2000). Collective Action and the Evolution of Social Norms, *Journal of Economic Perspectives* 14, 137–58.

Ostrom, E., Walker, J.M., and Gardner, R. (1992). Covenants with and without the Sword: Self-governance is Possible, *American Political Science Review* 86, 404–417.

Pagden, A. (1988). The Destruction of Trust and its Economic Consequences in the Case of Eighteenth-Century Naples, Chapter 8 in Gambetta (1988a) Chapter 8, pp. 127–141.

Putnam, R.D. (1993). *Making Democracy Work: Civic Traditions in Modern Italy*, Princeton: Princeton University Press. (With the collaboration of Robert Leonardi and Raffaella Y. Nonetti.)

Putnam, R.D. (2000). *Bowling Alone: The Collapse and Revival of American Community*, New York: Simon and Schuster.

Putterman, L. and Weil, D.N. (2010). Post-1500 Population Flows and The Long-Run Determinants of Economic Growth and Inequality, *Quarterly Journal of Economics* 125, 1627–1682.

Rabin, M. (1990), Communication Between Rational Agents, *Journal of Economic Theory* 51, 144–170.

Rabin, M. (1994). Cognitive Dissonance and Social Change, *Journal of Economic Behavior and Organization* 23, 177–194.

Radner, R. and Schotter, A. (1989). The Sealed-bid Mechanism: An Experimental Study, *Journal of Economic Theory* 48, 179–220.

Restuccia, D. and Rogerson, R. (2017). The Causes and Costs of Misallocation, *Journal of Economic Perspectives* 31, 151–174.

Riley, J. and Zeckhauser, R. (1983). Optimal Selling Strategies: When to Haggle, When to Hold Firm, *Quarterly Journal of Economics* 98, 267–289.

Rothschild, M. and Stiglitz, J.E. (1976). Equilibrium in Competitive Insurance Markets: An Essay on the Economics of Imperfect Information, *Quarterly Journal of Economics* 90, 630–649.

Rousseau, J.-J. (1755/1910). *Discourse on the Origin and Basis of Inequality Among Men*, English translation in C.W. Eliot (ed.), *Harvard Classics Volume 34: English and French Philosophers*, New York, NY: P.F. Collier & Son.

Rousseau, J.-J. (1762/1994). *The Social Contract*, English translation by Christopher Betts, World's Classics Series, Oxford: Oxford University Press.

Sally, D. (1995). Conversation and Cooperation in Social Dilemmas: A Metaanalysis of Experiments from 1958–1992, *Rationality and Society* 7, 58–92.

Satyanath, S., Voigtländer, N., and Voth, H.-J. (2017). Bowling for Fascism: Social Capital and the Rise of the Nazi Party, *Journal of Political Economy* 125, 478–526.

Savage, L.J. (1954). *The Foundations of Statistics*, New York: Dover.

Schelling, T.C. (1956). An Essay on Bargaining, *American Economic Review* 46, 281–306.

Schelling, T.C. (1960). *The Strategy of Conflict*, Cambridge: Harvard University Press.

Schipper, B.C. (2014). Unawareness – A Gentle Introduction to Both the Special Issue and the Literature, *Mathematical Social Sciences* 70, 1–9.

Schulz, J.F. (2022). Kin Networks and Institutional Development, *Economic Journal* 132, 2578–2613.

Schulz, J.F., Bahrami-Rad, D., Beauchamp, J.P., and Henrich, J. (2019). The Church, Intensive Kinship, and Global Psychological Variation, *Science* 366(6466).

Sethi, R. and Somanathan, E. (1996). The Evolution of Social Norms in Common Property Resource Use, *American Economic Review* 86, 766–788.

Shafir, E. and Tversky, A. (1992). Thinking through Uncertainty: Nonconsequential Reasoning and Choice, *Cognitive Psychology* 24, 449–474.

Shayo, M. (2009). A Model of Social Identity with an Application to Political Economy: National, Class and Redistribution, *American Political Science Review* 103, 147–174.

Shleifer, A. and Wolfenzon, D. (2002). Investor Protection and Equity Markets, *Journal of Financial Economics* 66, 3–27.

Silverman, D. (2004). Street Crime and Street Culture, *International Economic Review* 45, 761–786.

Skaperdas, S. (2006). Anarchy, *Oxford Handbook of Political Economy*, B. Weingast and D. Wittman (eds.), Oxford University Press.

Smith, A. (1759). *A Theory of Moral Sentiments*, printed for Andrew Millar, in the Strand; and Alexander Kincaid and J. Bell, in Edinburgh.

Sobel, J. (2005). Interdependent Preferences and Reciprocity, *Journal of Economic Literature*, 43, 392–436.

Spence, A.M. (1974). *Market Signaling*, Cambridge MA: Harvard University Press.

Tabellini, G. (2008). Institutions and Culture, *Journal of the European Economic Association* 6, 255–294.

Tabellini, G. (2010). Culture and Institutions: Economic Development in the Regions of Europe, *Journal of the European Economic Association* 8, 677–716.

Tajfel, H. and Turner, J.C. (1979). An Integrative Theory of

Intergroup Conflict, pp. 33–47 in W. G. Austin and S. Worchel (eds.), *The Social Psychology of Intergroup Relations*, Monterey, CA: Brooks/Cole.

Tannenbaum, D., Cohn, A., Zünd, C.L., and Maréchal, M.A. (2023). What Do Cross-country Surveys Tell Us About Social Capital? *Review of Economics and Statistics* forthcoming.

Tirole, J. (2001). Corporate Governance, *Econometrica* 69, 1–35.

Tirole, J. (2006). *The Theory of Corporate Finance*, Princeton, NJ: Princeton University Press.

Tirole, J. (2009). Cognition and Incomplete Contracts, *American Economic Review* 99, 265–294.

Townsend, R. (1979). Optimal Contracts and Competitive Markets with Costly State Verification, *Journal of Economic Theory* 21, 265–293.

Valley, K.L., Thompson, L., Gibbons, R., and Bazerman, M.H. (2002). How Communication Improves Efficiency in Bargaining Games, *Games and Economic Behavior* 38, 127–155.

Vanberg, C. (2008). Why Do People Keep Their Promises? An Experimental Test of Two Explanations, *Econometrica* 76, 1467–1480.

Watson, J., Miller, D.A., and Olsen, T.E. (2020). Relational Contracting, Negotiation, and External Enforcement, *American Economic Review* 110, 2153–2197.

Weber, M. (1905/1930). *The Protestant Ethic and the Spirit of Capitalism*, London: Allen & Unwin.

Weibull, J.W. (1995). *Evolutionary Game Theory*, Cambridge MA: MIT Press.

Welch, D. (1993). *Justice and the Genesis of War*, Cambridge MA: Cambridge University Press.

Wiggins, S.N. and Libecap, G.D. (1985). Oil Field Unitization: Contractual Failure in the Presence of Imperfect Information, *American Economic Review* 75, 368–385.

Williamson, O.E. (1971). Vertical Integration of Production: Market Failure Considerations, *American Economic Review, Papers and Proceedings* 61, 112–123.

Williamson, O.E. (1975). *Markets and Hierarchies*, New York: Free Press.

Williamson, O.E. (1985). *The Economic Institutions of Capitalism*, New York: Free Press.

Yamagishi, T. (1988). Exit from the Group as an Individualistic Solution to the Public Good Problem in the United States and Japan, *Journal of Experimental Social Psychology* 24, 530–542.

Yildiz M. (2003). Bargaining without a Common Prior: An Immediate Agreement Theorem, *Econometrica* 71, 793–811.

Yildiz M. (2011). Bargaining with Optimism, *Annual Review of Economics* 3, 451–478.

Young, H.P. (1993). Evolution of Conventions, *Econometrica* 61, 57–84.

Zahavi, A. (1975). Mate Selection – A Selection for a Handicap, *Journal of Theoretical Biology* 53, 205–214.

Index of Authors

222 Index of Authors

General Index

Printed and bound by CPI Group (UK) Ltd, Croydon, CR0 4YY

16/04/2025

14658410-0001